Enjoy

To Know He Is There

KIMBERLY LARRAINE

May this book help you to Know He is there for you Always!

Kimberly Larraine Seyboldt

Copyright © 2020 Kimberly Larraine

All rights reserved.

ISBN: 9798689171692

DEDICATION

To Jessica

CONTENTS

	Acknowledgments	i
	Introduction and Dedication	1
	Preface: A Journey	4
1	Planting the Seeds of Faith	6

~To Comfort and Protect You
~Six Hands upon My Head
~Planting My Seeds of Faith
~The Power of Prayer
~My Sister Eileen
~Jessica
~An Answer to Our Prayer

2	Seedlings Take Root with Angels Round About Me	24

~Angels in Disguise
~With God by My Side
~Character Building 101
~Tests, Tests and More Tests!
~A Circle of Friends
~The "Buddy" System
~Rich in the Things That Matter
~Please Help Us Find a New Home
~My Greatest Nursing Mentor
~Others Were Watching

3	A Tree Standing Tall In the Wind	52

~I Am Not So Far Away
~Spot
~A Letter from Tony
~Learning from One Another
~Promises
~A Change of Heart
~For Sammy
~The Challenge of Saying Goodbye

4   The Tree Bears Fruit   67
    ~Heavenly Insurance Premiums
    ~The Lord Chose My Assignment
    ~A Heavenly Intervention
    ~In the Right Place at the Right Time
    ~My Saving Grace
    ~Songs of the Heart
    ~Go Today
    ~I Just Thought I Would Call
    ~The Lay-Off
    ~Some of My Best Friends
    ~Unto the Least of These
    ~The Blessing
    ~A Most Amazing Conference Call
    ~Little Birds
    ~A Time and a Season
    ~"How Did You Know?"
    ~Stressful Bliss

5   Rays of Sunshine Through the Storm   112
    ~The Not So Innocent
    ~Florence Nightingale
    ~Nettie Jones
    ~Mrs. Sullivan

6   Not Without My Children   120
    ~Forced Family Fun (BJ)
    ~A Lesson from the Rib Cruncher
    ~Whatever...the Story of Kari
    ~For Sammy
    ~Run Like the Wind (James)
    ~A Chance to Know You (Meeting Dave)

7   Epilogue: To Know He Is There   137
    ~To Know He Is There
    ~A Prompting
    ~A Message from Tony
    ~Going Home

ACKNOWLEDGMENTS

My book would remain as small pieces of paper residing in a keepsake box had it not been for some very special people. A wonderful thank you to my children who were there to live through it all and allow me now to share it with others. To my sweet husband Mike who never once discouraged me, but instead told me my stories were worth sharing. To my editor Marian who wanted people to hear and be encouraged. Each time life threw me a curve, she kept working on my book. She has been more than my editor. She has been a teacher, my cheerleader and my friend. And most of all I need to acknowledge my Heavenly Father. Without his promptings and His faith in me, there would be no stories at all, no amazing miracles, or the daughter I turned out to be.

Note: Except where permission was given, the names in this book have been changed.

Cover and decorative divider: The cover was combined from two photos, the main one is by jplenio and the secondary one is by geralt. The decorative divider was created by GDJ. They can be found on Pixabay.

·

INTRODUCTION AND DEDICATION

For many years, strange and marvelous occurrences took place in my life. They happened so many times that I began to write them down on small pieces of paper. One by one, they took up residence in a keepsake box in the bottom of my dresser drawer. Most people would call these events mere coincidences. For the longest time, so did I...until the day Jessica passed away.

I will always remember the phone call I received at work from my sister Eileen. She was overwhelmed with grief as she told me that her husband Randie had found their daughter Jessica still and lifeless when he checked in on her that morning. My supervisor knew how close my sister and I were and immediately found another nurse to finish my shift.

So many thoughts filled my mind and touched my soul as I drove to my sister's home. I reflected on the day my own son passed away in a tragic car accident. My heart began aching for my sister. At the same time, I had great feelings of relief. Sweet little Jessica was free, and finally released from the endless hours of torment her body had been to her.

Jessica had been held prisoner from the moment of her delivery. The brain damage from lack of oxygen at the time of her birth was catastrophic. Jessica's emotional and physical development would be constrained for her entire earthly existence. Jessica weighed 55 pounds at age 21. She could not roll over. Never had she spoken a word. She was fed by her parents through a tube entering her stomach. During seizures, she would bite into one of her little fingers until it bled. Yet, Jessica was certainly aware of those around her, smiling when someone spoke to her.

I drove Randie and Eileen to the funeral home that afternoon, as they are both visually handicapped. The spirit was overwhelming as I entered the room to see Jessica. She lay calm and at peace. Without the repeated movements caused by her cerebral palsy, I saw her differently. For the first time I saw a beautiful young lady and I was in awe. I spoke to her, feeling that her spirit was near. I wept as I told her of my joy for her new life. I promised to stay close to her mother, as I knew Eileen would miss Jessica beyond comprehension. I carefully measured her frail mortal body to make her a beautiful burial dress. For all those moments, I knew I was in the presence of a celestial being. Tears flooded my eyes, for Jessica was home. Her mission on Earth had been completed.

Over the next several days, I felt especially close to the veil that parts this world from the next. I was prompted over and over in my mind about those little pieces of paper resting quietly in that bottom dresser drawer. Those feelings would not let my thoughts rest. Then an amazing thing happened. When I returned after a few days to lap swimming, Jessica's spirit felt even closer. Each little incident that I had written down became alive. Each one became a story. Soon, ladies were joining me in the jacuzzi to hear me record my stories on a small tape recorder.

"Did that really happen?" they asked.

Jessica would not let me rest. She would not let me forget.

"Aunt Kim!" she said, penetrating my heart. "Those were not coincidences. Father has been there all those times, in all that you have been through, remaining anonymous, while planting the seeds of faith."

So, it is to Jessica, that I dedicate this book.

To Our Jessica
Who never uttered a spoken word; yet, with her smile
Touched your heart, calmed your soul and let it be known
You were in the presence of an Angel

PREFACE: A JOURNEY

I once read a statement, a few years ago, that caught my eye. It went something like this: To gain wisdom, you must have experienced; and part of experience is making mistakes. I certainly liked that thought and it helped to strengthen the belief I have today, that life here upon the earth as we know it, is a journey. The paths we take and the choices we make along the way will help to mold our character and bring us one step closer to the person we are to become.

The book you are about to read is a spiritual one, for the greatest thing that I have come to know is that we were not sent here upon the earth to make that journey alone. I know to the inner depths of my soul that I am a child of a loving and caring Heavenly Father. He created me in spirit before he sent me here in flesh. He knew which family he would send me to. He knows my truest nature, and as I walk through life, He hopes I will make those choices that will ultimately bring me home to Him.

I am the mother of six and grandmother to several times as many. My heart is happy when my children are doing well. I share their sorrow when they are hurting and being challenged. I am there when they ask for help and reach out for guidance. That is what a parent does. That's the love that our Heavenly

Parent shows us as well.

My life so far has been an amazing journey. The greatest and most marvelous truth (or Wisdom) I have acquired was not in the books I studied to become a nurse, but during the trials I faced at that time. Heavenly Father was there every step of the way. He is real, and He is loving. He is very forgiving. Each time I stumbled and fell, He was there to pick me up. He gave me hope when I was in despair and encouragement when I felt I could not continue. My Father in Heaven answered my prayers in such literal ways that I knew He was by my side. There were times of such profound sorrow, when I could not push Satan's grip of hopelessness away, that Father threw his loving arms around me and would not let go. He took upon His shoulders the heavy burdens that I could not handle at times and let me carry what I could.

To this day, my children remember and marvel at how our prayers were answered. We often knelt together. They knew my worries and shared my concerns. They were amazed as God blessed us so literally and quickly with the things we needed. This is what my story is about. The greatest gift I could ever give my children is to teach them that their Father in Heaven is real. That is what I hope each reader will come to understand. Every story is true. I would not have given up one trial in exchange for the experience that it gave me. I hope you will discover, as I did for myself, that it is often not until after the trial of our faith, that we come to understand what the tribulation was for, and in some cases, that knowledge may not come right away. Know that there is Someone there to help you...Always. And know that the person you are to become will never be measured by your trials, but by the way you endure, challenge by challenge, and one step at a time.

Know that He is there

1 PLANTING THE SEEDS OF FAITH

*Coincidences are God's way of letting you know
He is there.*

Just as small seeds are planted into the ground, with the hope of a beautiful garden, so too are our seeds of faith. One day after another and one spiritual happening after another, small memories like seedlings are planted into rich soil. They are planted deep into our hearts to be a testimony of God's goodness. Then in those times of trial and struggle as we wonder if we can make it one more day, we see our tiny seedlings lifting their heads, breaking through the earth. We come to realize that while we could not see Mother Nature's handiwork until that moment, it was happening day by day. My seedlings were planted, and nurtured by kind and loving friends, my caring family and by the greatest gardener of all, my eternal Heavenly Father.

To Comfort and Protect You

I was only four years old when I became keenly aware that I had not been sent to this Earth to complete my journey alone. Born into chaos, my home was often filled with loud voices and parents who quarreled intensely and often. I honestly do not think that my parents understood the fear and confusion I felt at that age. I know I was extremely sensitive as a child and their frequent arguments would send me running from life's turmoil to my quiet place. Grabbing our dog Shorty, I would run to the backyard swing, there gliding slowly while cuddling my poor doggie for comfort and solace. I pulled back and forth until I could feel a rhythm. I would then sing. Mind you, those four-year-old legs could not push us high. They did not need to, for it was the motion and the rhythm that mattered most.

The dog never once protested. He was my captive audience of one. I loved to sing. My voice must not have been disturbing, for he sat on my lap, oh so still. I did not realize then what I have come to understand now: these sweet, short Sunday school songs, sung verse by verse, were like prayers. They were offered up tenderly, and sung earnestly, searching for comfort and a way to calm my soul. Like the slow-moving pendulum of the clock, the soft flowing rhythm calmed my heart and allowed for a most wonderful companion to be by my side. Though I could still hear voices in the distance, they became muted, as the arms I longed for wrapped me and my puppy into a safe world. I felt an encompassing, yet gentle power round about me. It uplifted my spirit and made me feel loved.

As the years passed, I came to long for that wonderful

power to be my constant companion. It was only through that power, that God put me in a position to know of those in my life who needed help. That same power protected me many times from harm, even so much as to guide me to safe havens. Through promptings, and on some occasions, a shove, He would guide me to those in trouble. He would guide me to people searching to find their way back to Him. My life became amazing, and I often said, "I can't believe what just happened!"

You are never here on this Earth to journey alone. Heavenly Father is always there to protect and guide you. He wants to comfort you. When there is a beautiful song in your heart, you invite Him in. He is a most wonderful loving Father, and He has given me my most cherished gift: the gift of the Holy Ghost.

And the remission of sins bringeth meekness, and lowliness of heart; and because of meekness and lowliness of heart cometh the visitation of the Holy Ghost, which Comforter filleth with hope and perfect love, which love endureth by diligence unto prayer, until the end shall come, when all the saints shall dwell with God.
Moroni 8:26

Six Hands Upon My Head

My family lived in a new little sub-division in Magna Utah when I was about seven. They had gone through many trials from the time they had first moved there. My sister Eileen had to have surgery to remove her eye because of severe glaucoma. My baby brother Brent had been born with a severe congenital heart defect. Except for some anemia and a mouth full of crowns, my health had not been a scare to them. Then suddenly, one weekend, that changed.

I woke up with an incredible rash from head to toe. I felt extremely ill. Besides being so hot with a fever, the thing I remember most was how the light hurt my eyes. It was the first time I had heard the word "quarantine." I had the measles; and not the simple three-day measles known as rubella. I could not eat. I did not want so much as a Popsicle. Then my fever began to climb alarmingly high. Fifty-some years later, I can still remember how I heard voices all around me. I remember how they seemed distant and I did not know who was there. What I do remember was hearing my dad's voice saying, "Sis, some men from church are here to give you a blessing." All my mother had to do was phone our neighbor, Dr. Hill. When she told him how high my fever was, the blessing came first, and quickly. It was as though Dr. Hill had pulled the men right out of his little black medical bag. My bed was surrounded by those who took no concern for their own health. It was surrounded by love. I remember the coolness of their hands. I remember them saying my given name. What followed is what I remember the most. Their voices faded, like they do when you go under anesthesia for surgery. I quickly fell into a deep, deep sleep that lasted for two days. Though my fever broke instantly, I did not wake up. My parents knew that I would be ok because that was the promise given in the blessing.

Even after two days of rest, it took several more for the light to stop hurting my eyes and to once again, relish Popsicles. My recovery was bittersweet as my energy returned and I desired to play. I wanted to be with friends again, but I think they were worried that their hair might start to fall out like mine soon did. Just a temporary set-back for it grew back thicker than ever. What was far more important to me, was knowing that when Heavenly Father makes a promise, he keeps it.

It is never the trial you face, that will prove who you are. It is, however, the way you face your trial that will prove what you are to become.

Planting My Seeds of Faith

My seeds of faith were planted in my heart as I began listening to the account of my grandmother's childhood which took place more than 50 years before I was born.

I lived close to my grandmother for the first eight years of my life. Grandma stood barely five feet tall, yet, with her German accent, and distinct power of conviction, I viewed her as a strong and powerful lady. Grandma was never afraid to offer her opinion, so if you didn't want a lecture, you chose your subjects of conversation carefully. There was never a guess as to which side of the fence she sat. She was also a wonderful cook. She sewed beautifully. The thing I will always remember most about this sweet lady is how often she expressed herself and the love for her family. From the time I was old enough to understand, Grandma spoke of her childhood and the marvelous experiences that had their part in making her the woman she became.

Grandma was born in 1894 and was the oldest of five living children. She told me how she lived in Stettin in North Germany (now a part of Poland). Her family was poverty-stricken and lived in row apartment houses. Her mother had to work, so it was her grandparents who took care of her during the day. I remember her telling me how excited her family was when missionaries came to their door to share the gospel. From that day on, her parents had a burning desire to be baptized and go to America to live in Salt Lake City. They sold their furniture and belongings to have enough money for passage on a boat. Unfortunately, a smallpox epidemic grounded their hopes during the fall they were to emigrate. They were quarantined. Grandma tells how they had to use their passage money to live on until the quarantine was lifted.

I am a grandmother now myself. My heart breaks as I remember grandma telling us how she cried on the train ride to reach the boat. Her own grandmother loved her and kissed her and told her, "I'll never see you again." She told us she never forgot that last "Good-bye."

It is grandma's account of what happened to their little family from the time they got off the boat that makes me realize the strength and courage my great-grandparents possessed. They did not have the $100 needed to get to Salt Lake City from Boston Harbor because of the smallpox epidemic. Their ticket read Piedmont Wyoming. To make matters worse, they did not have the $50 necessary to show the Immigration Officer. The missionaries loaned them the money needed, so they could get off the boat in America.

"Mr. Stelter," said the officer, "what are you going to do here in America, with only $50 and this little family?"

It was my great-grandmother that spoke up strongly in her German accent. "We Work!" she said, and the officer let them go ahead.

They landed in Piedmont, Wyoming at midnight. They had been on the train for five days and five nights. They were put up in one room in a hotel. They went to bed hungry and tired. They spent a week there, then found another place to live. They were directed to an old, one-room log cabin that had no beds or furniture or fireplace. I cannot imagine what I would have done if I were in their place, with my six little ones. Their baby was just two months old.

To go such a distance with no money, no food, no job and a language barrier was certainly incredible. Grandma told me that the next day, they were given a few boards to build a bunk in each corner. Great-grandma sewed together gunny sacks, so that hay and straw could be placed into them. Their only box full of dishes and bedding became their table. An old stove without a damper became their warmth and oven. Grandma told about their first meal, brought by gracious neighbors. Oatmeal! Oatmeal and fresh milk! Never had anything tasted so good.

Great-grandpa got a job on the railroad. Great-grandma took in wash from the railroad workers. My grandmother and her little brothers carried water from the hotel a block away all day long for the wash tub. Grandma remembers playing with horny toads in the sagebrush by day and listening to the howling of the coyotes at their door during the night. The hard work did not matter. They were in America! Piedmont, Wyoming was just the beginning.

I would think back to my grandmother's story and her life yet to come. It became my strength. Grandma was the mother of ten children. She became a widow when her youngest was only two. I never knew my maternal grandfather. My youngest has his eyes. Another child has his stature. I did come to know my grandmother, however. She remained strong in the gospel. She was an incredible cook and seamstress. She worked at many jobs to put food on the table for her children. I had no idea that watching her sacrifices while she was alive would become a source of strength for me when she was gone. I did not know back then of the trials I would face in my future. I do know that I felt her loving presence on many occasions when I did not know how I was to support my own little family or myself. And with a smile, I put on new courage, remembering the seeds of faith planted in my heart with those resounding words, "We Work!"

Seedlings take their root from knowing of God's miracles.

The Power of Prayer

I cannot tell you the story of my sister Eileen without first telling you a story of my parents. My mother and father were both the ninth children to be born in their respective families. Dad was a country boy whose family heritage is anchored in Chewelah, Washington. The cattle ranch on which he was raised was established from homesteading. Mom, on the other hand, was a city girl who spent her first 15 years in Salt Lake City. My Dad was painfully shy, but as Mom told the story, it was she who converted him into the fun-loving and friendly man we all knew. They were married in 1949. As their life together unfolded, they were blessed to find out that their twosome would soon be three.

Excitement about the event was soon overshadowed by my mother's perpetual waves of nausea. She succumbed to retching every morning, and it soon became clear, my mother could keep nothing in her stomach. Days passed into weeks and as one month ended and another began, the story was the same. Before long, my mother had lost 60 pounds. She was but a whisper of her former self and soon had to be hospitalized. To her doctor's surprise, she did not miscarry.

This was an extremely stressful time in my parents' lives. They lived in a small one-bedroom house on Eighth West in Salt Lake City, Utah. Dad worked for the Otto Buehner Company, making only $1.08 an hour. With a hospital bill mounting, they worried how they were going to survive.

When Mom and Dad went for a visit to Spokane Washington, Mom told us how her sister Lavon cried. Mom was nothing but skin and bones, yet the baby continued to survive. The first thing my mother was able to keep on her stomach with much success were her sister's homemade sour pickles. Near the time of my sister's arrival, my mother had gained back only five pounds of the 60 she had lost.

Eileen made her entrance into the world early in the morning on April 27, 1951. Dad told of how excited they were to see their little six-pound daughter with a full head of wavy, brown hair. The excitement quickly disappeared as they held her close. The doctor saw it also. The room grew silent. Opaque clouds covered not one, but both of her corneas. Eileen had been born blind.

"She will never be able to see," their doctor pronounced.

The opaque clouds covering each eye would not allow the pupils to be seen. The light could not enter her eyes. And so, it was. And so, it would be. The only explanation that could be voiced was that her eyes did not have enough moisture to develop properly due to Mom's severe dehydration and weight loss.

My parents made regular trips to the eye specialist, but the prognosis was always the same. She would see only shadows of light and dark during her lifetime. Grandma cried. Each time she rocked Eileen to sleep, she would cry, "my baby, my baby."

Mom and Dad were told that Eileen would most likely need to go to a school for the blind. My parents were aware that this might be in Eileen's future. She was normal in every other way, crawling as most babies do, cooing when cuddled. They knew she would not stay little forever.

Month by month she grew. She was a pretty little thing, always happy and smiling. My parents' hearts were breaking. Grandma was devastated. When Eileen was six months old, Grandma encouraged my parents to exercise their faith. They decided to all petition Heavenly Father about this sweet little girl. They were members of a church that embraced fasting and prayer. All the congregations in the surrounding area set aside a weekend to have a special fast and prayer for Eileen. My parents and others pleaded to the Lord with heart-felt words, "Please Father, please help her if it is your will." The fast ended. Day after day passed by but nothing changed.

Nearly one week went by. My parents watched little Eileen as she pulled herself up to stand at the coffee table, as she often did. This time, though, they noticed something different. Something had changed. As they watched, Dad could see that her movements were more purposeful. She reached out for things as she had never done before, with purpose, as if reaching for something she saw. Could it be? Mom told of how she picked up my sister and there, that day, in her left eye, not in the middle, but off to the side was. a pupil.

Dr. Sontag cried as he examined her. There was just no explanation of how it happened. But there it was, the whisper of a pupil. Eileen never regained sight in her right eye and in fact, had it removed because of severe headaches caused by glaucoma at the age of eight. She is now legally blind but sees far more than mere shadows.

Eileen was never sent to a school for the blind. She was however sent to the University of Washington at age 18 to attend a class on how to live with a handicap in a sighted world. Funny how the Lord works his miracles—or should I say his coincidences—for her husband-to-be was taking the same class. How that twosome became three and then four and eventually eight...well now, that story might just take a few more chapters.

My Sister Eileen

I have always felt that those who come to this Earth with physical and mental challenges are great in the eyes of our beloved Heavenly Father. I also feel that it was their decision to accept such a challenge before entering this life. Their struggles and trials would not only prove further who they already are in Spirit, but also be a source of strength and growth for those around them.

Many of the names have been changed in my book to provide confidentiality. This chapter is different. The name is unchanged. This chapter is dedicated to my sister Eileen. Her story is real. She is the person who has had the most influence in strengthening my faith and helping me to spiritually grow. I have felt that Father in Heaven placed certain children in my care to keep me uplifted during my hardest times. There is no doubt in my mind that I was placed in a family with a sister like Eileen to temper the person I could become and gently mold me into the person Heavenly Father wanted me to be.

Eileen was just shy two days from being a year old when I was born. My mother's doctor had encouraged her to have another child, so she would not continue to dwell on the misfortune of having a handicapped baby. I was not the pretty brown-haired baby that Eileen had been. I was pasty and bald and, to make matters worse, I was colicky. I cried if you picked me up. I cried if you put me down. I cried if you even looked at me. I think, for my parents, it was a glimpse of what was to come. I would always be finding a way to make myself known. Eileen was the sweet one, so meek and unselfish. I, on the other hand, was deplorable. I would encourage my sister to get into mischief as my partner–in–crime, but I could always run faster and, because she could not see Dad coming, "the switch" would always find her legs first. Eileen and I looked more and more alike as we grew older. Her brown hair changed to match my blonde wavy hair (when it finally decided to make its appearance). We were always about the same height, until I passed her by in pubescence. We were a twosome. We shared the same room. She liked blue. I preferred pink. We did everything together, so it didn't seem to unravel me much when I noticed other people staring at her eyes. As far as I was concerned, they had never matched. I knew Eileen as my sister and best friend. I never thought of her much as my big sister, though, for I was the one who took the lead. I helped her find things, kept her from stumbling. I described things to her when they were too far away for her to see. When we were four and five, a button popped off her dress and landed in front of her on the floor.

"Where is my button?" she said. "I can't see it."

It was at that moment, that I truly realized what her visual limitations were.

When Eileen was about five, nearing six, she started having headaches. They became more and more severe as each month passed. She did not want to play as much. She complained about the light on bright days or when she would enter a bright room. The headaches became so painful that she lost her appetite and started losing weight. Our pediatrician was at a loss to know what was wrong. Our Aunt Lavon in Washington wondered if it might be Eileen's eyes that were causing the problem. Aunt Lavon had worked for a doctor in Salt Lake City a few years earlier. It was his son who was a new ophthalmologist there in Salt Lake City where my parents lived. His name was Dr. White. He recognized the problem within minutes of examining Eileen. He diagnosed Eileen with severe glaucoma. Eileen could not see in her right eye at all and that was the eye that had so much pressure in it. Her eye had to be removed!

How do you tell an eight-year-old child that she would have only one eye? My sister has since shared with me how frightening all the examinations were because she could not see what they were doing. Going into surgery produced profound anxiety for her. To this day her heart races and her hands become clammy when I take her for an eye exam.

The Doctor warned my parents that removal of her eye would be extremely painful after the surgery and to be prepared for a difficult recovery. My parents were soon to know of just how much pain Eileen had endured before her operation, for when she was asked post-operatively, how she was feeling, she sweetly conceded, "Mommy, I didn't know I could feel so good."

I became an especially good friend for my sister during those next few months. She was labeled with malicious names. Eileen just took it in stride as she heard "Patched eye pirate!" or "One-eyed Monster!" The names were nothing in comparison to the headaches she had endured.

I have always been amazed at my sister's ability to handle change. Changing from one school to another during middle school was most difficult for me. I can only imagine how hard it was for her. Eileen never did attend a blind school and it was our parents who were instrumental in making sure that Eileen was able to attend public school. They fought to have readers and special classmates take down her assignments from the board, so she might read them later. We were able to attend the same high school for all four years. It was during this time, that I realized how amazing my sister was. She had excellent grades. She has a wonderful sense of humor, and so did many of her handicapped friends. I remember how blind Ben once asked her out.

"Would you like to go on a blind date? I'm really out of sight!"

And I will never forget the day of my first car accident, the beginning day of my sophomore year. She was my passenger as I accidentally backed into someone in the student parking lot.

"You're on your own," she sneered, " I didn't see a thing."

I watched her take rejection with such grace. We both tried out for Acapella Choir the same year. I was so excited to rush home and share my acceptance into the choir. It lost all meaning when I found out that Eileen had not. They did not think she would be able to sight-read new music. They did not know my sister. She has a beautiful voice. It was one of the several disappointments that my sister would face over the years. She would never, however, let you see her disappointment. My heart ached knowing there were things she would never be able do. She would never take a driver's test. She would never see the beautiful colors of a sunset, or a bird perched in a tree. There are so many things we take for granted. She cannot see the menu at a drive-up or see all the stars twinkling at night. She cannot see the beauty of the ocean at a distance.

In all of her adversity, Eileen has been blessed. My parents insisted that she take a class at the University of Washington for training for the blind. She protested, but it was to her advantage that she lost that argument, for it was there that she met her wonderful husband Randie. He was there to take the same class. It wasn't long before she knew love, and not much longer before she experienced Motherhood.

You would think that Eileen had experienced more tribulation than any one person should in their lifetime, but that was not to be the case with my sister. More was yet to come, for Heavenly Father, in his infinite wisdom was to bless Randie and Eileen with their cherished daughter, Jessica.

> For He shall give His angels charge over thee,
> to keep thee in all thy ways. Psalm 91:11

Jessica

Jessica was sent to this Earth on September 27, 1978. She joined Eileen and Randie's family of four little daughters, making it five. I would be remiss if I did not dedicate this chapter to her for it was at her bidding, from beyond the veil, that I was prompted to put my stories of faith into words and onto paper.

Her chapter in this life begins in Medford, Oregon. Though her earthly account would include only a few chapters, it would touch the hearts of many and bring us hope for years to come. Eileen had chosen to give birth at a hospital several miles from their home, as that is where her obstetrician had hospital privileges. Laboring for most of the morning, Eileen knew the delivery of their baby was getting closer. They arrived at the hospital and all was going well, and she welcomed hearing the words, "It's time to Push!" Soon the doctor could see the baby had lots of hair. With a couple more pushes, her head was delivered. It is usually at this time, and with a couple of more hard pushes, that a baby makes its way into the world. This was not to be the case with our sweet little Jessica. Her head had been delivered, but her shoulders would not slip through. She was caught! All known methods were tried there in the delivery room for almost 20 minutes to bring her into this world. Eileen was in terrible pain. The room was tense. As Jessica finally slipped through, the room was filled with fast acting doctors and nurses. There is a name for this type of complication. It is called "shoulder dystocia." Jessica was cyanotic and blue. It was Eileen and Randie's friend Brad who received the distress call. He was a nurse anesthesiologist and when he arrived, all efforts were being taken to revive Jessica. To everyone's amazement, she took that first breath of life and survived. Randie and Eileen were only allowed to see their new baby daughter for a brief moment, then she was quickly whisked away, and taken by ambulance to Rogue Valley Medical Center in Medford. They stabilized Eileen quickly so that she and Randie could join Jessica.

It was a sad day for everyone. When Eileen and Randie touched Jessica in her incubator, they could feel the movement of her body as she began to seize. Although no one knew it at the time, Jessica would live a life with many seizures yet to come. Her spirit would be held prisoner in a frail body that would never allow her to roll over, sit or stand.

Randie and Eileen moved to Portland and closer to family, so that we could help. It was so very difficult for them both. Jessica looked like any normal baby. She did however have difficulty with nursing. It was so sad to watch my sister. One month passed into another. My heart broke as each milestone in Jessica's development was not met. My sister never lost hope. She watched as I had my last baby less than a year after Jessica's birth. She watched as my baby Bjarne progressed, and her Jessica did not.

Jessica had many seizures. So much of her brain had been destroyed. We made thumb guards for her fingers as she would sometimes have a seizure and bite her little fingers to the bone. Many people suggested to Eileen that she should put Jessica in "The Providence Child Care Center." I remember to this day what Eileen once said to me.

"I know with all my heart, why Heavenly Father restored some of my sight to me. He was going to give me Jessica. What better person to take care of a handicapped child than a handicapped person like myself? I know what it will mean for her. I know what it is like to be handicapped."

Many times, I felt guilty because I was thankful to be going through my set of trials which seemed so small in comparison. Later Eileen confessed to me that she would never trade her trials for mine. The Lord knows us. He knows what we can endure. He knows what trials can make us strong.

Jessica—just like her mother—was a pretty, little thing. Although she never spoke, she smiled when you talked to her. There was never a way to know how much she understood, for she could not express her feelings in words. It took hours to feed Jessica because she constantly rolled food back at you with her tongue. She was frail and could not gain weight. At the age of eight, a feeding tube was placed in her abdomen. Even with the feeding tube, her body could tolerate only so much food. High calorie liquid supplements would cause their own set of problems. Jessica's arms were in perpetual motion, reaching out in front of her. She rarely flexed her knees.

Jessica was a gift of love to her family. Everyone shared in feeding her and spending time with her. Her siblings were sweet and loving. My children were also taught lessons on love through this sweet little girl. The word "retard" was never to be used in our home. My children witnessed firsthand what handicapped people go through. My children had noticed that Aunt Eileen's eyes were different. They looked beyond the flesh. They all love her warm, giving spirit. To this day, I do not know how my sister was able to give so much.

Randie and Eileen had their final child, a son, whom they named Lance. When Lance became older, he came to know that angels are close by. Eileen shared with me a wonderful occurrence that was incredibly special for Lance.

When Lance was eight-years-old, he shared a room with Jessica for she was so small she slept in a crib. On this special evening, Lance was awoken from sleep. Their room was engulfed with light. He became frightened as he saw an entity standing above the floor leaning over Jessica's crib. He could see that this personage, dressed in a white robe, was tenderly stroking Jessica's head, as to give her comfort. He was frightened, as any eight-year-old would be, and put his covers over his head. The being was there when he took another glance. Running to Eileen and Randie's room, his experience was dismissed as a dream. When he was ushered back to bed, the entity was gone. Lance continues to hold this experience in his heart, for it would serve as an anchor for his belief in a loving Heavenly Father and His gift of compassion and protection. Lance knew then, and believes now, that his sister was wrapped in the arms of love.

Jessica never weighed more than 55 pounds. Our hearts broke as a phone call came to us one early summer morning. Jessica had passed gently away in her sleep over night. She was gone. She did not live to see her 22nd birthday. I went to help my sister and we went to see her together. She was so beautiful. Without the continual motions of her hands moving about, I saw her so differently. She was at peace. Her trial was over. Her body no longer held her captive. She was free. I have no doubt, that on that wonderful morning, Jessica was greeted by many of those who loved her. I am sure she was wrapped in the arms of love by her welcoming Savior and Heavenly Father.

An Answer to Our Prayer

Prayer is such a powerful force and when combined with faith, amazing things can happen. I will never forget that evening, over 30 years ago. My husband was a new convert to The Church of Jesus Christ of Latter-Day Saints, so we had to wait a year before we could be sealed for time and all eternity in the beautiful Salt Lake City Temple. We had invited my sister and her husband to go along with us. We all went in the same car. It was a long drive from Portland, Oregon to Salt Lake City, especially with our four little children, two of them just babies.

The road was dark, with few streetlights to shine on the path that led up and over the winding mountain pass. As we neared the mountain's summit, the lights on our car began to flicker. Within a few moments, the flickering stopped, and we had no working head lights at all. There we were on a cold September evening, high on a mountain top, and no way to see far enough ahead to make our descent downward. When all efforts to get a better connection to the lights had failed, our husbands both agreed that it was time for a prayer. My brother-in-law's voice was calm and reassuring as he asked Heavenly Father simply and most sincerely to help us down the steep mountain pass.

We waited for about 15 minutes, full of anxiety, yet full of hope, when a car slowly came up behind us. When they saw we had no lights, they went around us and got right in front of our car, helping us slowly down the steep and winding road. They did not get out of their car to ask us about our dilemma. We were so grateful to follow their wonderful glowing taillights all the way down the treacherous patch of highway. Near the bottom of the hill, our escort slowly pulled into a long driveway. We followed close behind them. A lady got out of the car. To our amazement she became startled as we got out of ours, for you see, she never realized that we had followed her all the way down the mountain. She did not realize we were behind her at all. She was much too preoccupied. She was looking for her little lost dog. She had driven that winding road several times that day trying to find her lost, and much-loved companion. We knew that she had been an answer to our prayer. She told us how she was in her pajamas and ready to retire, when she felt prompted to try—one last time—to find her pup.

While our husbands were fixing the car's lights, our children enjoyed some hot chocolate and we all exchanged addresses. We were happy upon arriving back home to learn that her dog had returned. And remembering that eventful night, we were all grateful that Heavenly Father had helped us all to be one step closer to our eternal destination. For each of us, that evening planted in our hearts the love of a Father who had sent a most welcomed answer to our prayer.

2 SEEDLINGS TAKE ROOT WITH ANGELS ROUND ABOUT ME

...faith is things which are hoped for and not seen; wherefore, dispute not because ye see not, for ye receive no witness until after the trial of your faith.
Ether 12:6

The most difficult time of my life happened nearly four decades ago, but the memory of it will never fade. It was a time of great hardship. It was a time of wonderful miracles. It was the time when my roots of faith became securely anchored. Repeated reliance on the powers of heaven would anchor my being so strongly that I could not be uprooted. I knew I was loved and soon began to blossom into the person my Father knew I could become.

Angels in Disguise

Heavenly Father is saddened, I am sure, when one of his

sons or daughters ends the unity of their family because of divorce. The situation is even more far-reaching when there are children involved. Most children not only lose the close contact of one of their parents, but many times will have to move and often are put into childcare for the first time. A choice to divorce is a decision that will affect each member of that family for years to come.

I never imagined that divorce was a path that my life was to take, especially after bringing six little individuals into this world, but it did. My chapters are not to place blame, for my book is one of hope. These next few chapters are to show you how kind and forgiving our Father in Heaven is. He sent each one of us to this earth to experience life. He knows that we will all make mistakes. He hopes that we will never have to experience the pain of divorce, but he will be close by in case we do.

It was over 35 years ago that I found out for myself just how loving Father in Heaven can be. It was in November. I had stayed behind with our six children in Portland to sell our home. The decision to separate came less than two weeks after moving to The Dalles to join my husband. The gravity of the situation soon set in when I realized there would be no way to purchase the home we were staying in and there was no home to go back to. Things became worse. The house was cold, and the gas heat was too expensive. It was a terrible week. All my little ones were getting colds, and our car sounded the same. It coughed and sputtered just like the kids. You would think that a broken marriage, a few steps from homelessness, sick kids, and a cranky car would be enough. I guess I was not humble enough though, for more was yet to come. I needed to go to the pharmacy to pick up medicine for my sick baby. I asked my oldest son Tony to start the car and get it warmed up, so it wouldn't leave me stranded somewhere. Being just 12, he was always happy to pretend he was the driver, even though he was just the driver of a motionless car. Oh, I remember that cold bitter evening well! Tony came into the house telling me the car was ready. It was a dark night. The curb was only 15 feet from our outside stairs. I told my son I would be right there, but he was there to meet me at the front door.

"Mom, the car is gone."

He was upset and crying, for he had left the keys in the car, the car that was headed for Idaho as we later learned. The car sputtered its last cough there. The angry thief smashed all its windows out in retaliation.

I was so blue and so depressed. I was also angry that someone could be so bold! I still needed the medicine for my baby, so I went across the backyard alley to John and Donna's. They were members of my church. John was the realtor for the home I was staying in. Donna had become my first and dearest friend in this unfamiliar city. She was truly kind. She had four little ones of her own, but she was happy to help me out. I shared my frustration with her. She listened as only a true friend could.

I went to my bedroom that dismal night wondering just what I had done to be the recipient of such bad misfortune. I knelt beside my bed, wondering what might lie ahead, and asked the Lord for help. With no more tears to cry, I finally drifted off to sleep.

It was the beginning of the next day that would welcome the spark of hope. I had just sent the older kids off to school. Soon there was a knock on the door. There was a friend from my church to give assistance. We all help each other in our church and that day was to be no exception. I will never forget her. She had beautiful white hair. An uplifting aura surrounded her. She listened to my concerns for my children. She could see that I was anxious and worried. What she did next was the turning point in my life. She grabbed me by the hand and asked if I had a large mirror. Together we traveled into the bathroom.

Standing behind me she said, "Look into the mirror. Tell me what you see." Before I could answer, she spoke again.

"This is a beautiful daughter of a loving and kind Heavenly Father. He wants to help her, and He wants her to succeed. Get to know this lady in the mirror. Talk to her. Help lift her up. What happens to this lady and her children is going to be up to her. She can succeed. Father wants her to. He will never leave her."

Before the end of her visit we had explored things I could do. They were the things I was already doing, things I would continue to do until I could get back home. Additionally, she encouraged me to take in sewing, take in orders for homemade rolls and set up daycare to help meet my family's needs. Then she took a food order to make sure our shelves were filled until I could make money on my own. I have thought of her so many times. I wonder if I would have become a nurse had it not been for her, there in my home, that day.

Later that afternoon, I had another visitor stop by. John came by and returned my portion of the earnest money that had been put down on the house for its purchase. He said I could rent the home until it had another buyer. That was an exceptionally kind thing to do since he had his own little family to support.

"Please," he said, "go to Portland for the holidays and buy yourself another car and be with your family." And so I did. That money was bus fare to Portland and a down payment on the "Blue Bomb" as we called her. Light blue and ugly, she would be our transportation for three difficult years.

Now the generosity did not end there. We spent that Christmas in Portland with family. We returned to The Dalles to find a foot of snow. We also came home to the most wonderful Christmas gift of all. My kids, eager to play with John and Donna's kids, cut across the alley that separated our homes from one another.

My son Jimmy returned quickly through our back-door exclaiming, "Mom, you have got to come and see our backyard!"

While we were gone, the leader of our congregation had enlisted the help of his eight sons. They had delivered several cords of wood with lots of it split into kindling. That kindling helped start the fires that kept our large Schrader woodstove going through all the winter and into the spring, keeping daycare kids warm, homemade bread rising, and the lady in the mirror warm as she mended clothes for her neighbors.

Do I believe in angels? Yes, I do. Some are beyond the veil of this earth, but others are right here among us, to be sure.

With God by My Side

My Heavenly Father is real. He knows me personally. He created my spirit and through the wonderful creation of man, He made it possible for me to have my body. He also gives to each person, the potential for a successful life. He gives to each individual special talents and traits. And to each person He gives the gifts of hope and faith. I believe that these two special gifts, when used together, allow us to become the person that only our loving Heavenly Father knows we can be. They are inseparable. When we find ourselves at our lowest moments, many of us find comfort in believing the possibility that our lives will change for the better. For many, hope begins there and ends there. When I add faith to hope, things begin to change. When I place confidence and trust in the hands of my Father, all things become possible. So much of my life has been based on faith. As you place your trust in Heavenly Father and serve Him first, above all worldly considerations, He will bless you. He has blessed me so many times, in such literal ways, that I have come to know He is always by my side.

Satan would have different plans for my life, of that, I am certain. There I was at age 30, with him trying to make me feel ashamed about my choices in life up to that point. What kind of a person was I, after all? Look at all my mistakes. I was a high school dropout and mother at 17. I had tried some college courses and failed most of them. I not only married the wrong person but allowed five more children to come into my miserable mess. By age 30, I was divorced, one step away from homelessness, and then, not only responsible for myself, but six little ones, the smallest barely walking. Satan also knew me and how fragile I was back then. He was so prepared to enter my thoughts and take over my way of thinking. The choices he wanted me to make would negatively last for generations to come. He desired my children to feel engulfed in poverty, with no way out, perhaps to hand despair on down to their little ones.

"He is right," I said to myself, repeatedly.

Many nights right after my divorce, I would be awakened by a feeling of impending doom, a feeling so despairing, that I came to know that Satan is very real. Looking back now, I realize that his powerful spirit knew what Heavenly Father had planned for me and wanted in every way to prevent it from happening.

It was at that time that I asked for a blessing. I felt at war with this powerful adversary. It was bad enough to have him enter my thoughts by day, but to have him try to overcome my spirit while I lay sleeping was frightening. The missionaries in my church placed loving hands upon my head one special Sunday afternoon. I felt a powerful and calming force uplift my spirit that day, as a blessing of healing and comfort was given to me. I was promised health. I was promised that the power of the Holy Ghost would be with me if I would pray often. I was counseled to go back to school, that all my needs would be met if I would have faith in my Heavenly Father. My blessing ended with the acknowledgement that Father in Heaven was aware of my dilemma and little family. I was told of His desire to see me happy and successful. I was promised that my life would be like those of his Apostles, that my every need would be provided for, all being based on my faith and diligence. I was told that angels were nearby to watch over me and my little ones. I was told to never lose hope, to always have faith. As the missionaries' hands left my head, and the tears rolled down my cheeks, I knew that Satan would be kept at bay as I drew closer to my Heavenly Father. That afternoon was to be the first day of the rest of my life. From that moment on, I testify to you, that I never felt afraid again. I knew that I had been given wonderful promises. I felt the love of my Savior and Heavenly Father.

From that day on, I did not want to disappoint them. I could not imagine that afternoon how I was going to make it through school with a large family, no money, and only a dream. The next three years were to prove to my repeated astonishment that God's promises are sure, as sure as His love and kindness.

Character Building 101

To understand the extent of Heavenly Father's promises on that special day, you must first come to appreciate the person I was back in 1982. I was the newly divorced mother of six children, ages 18 months to 12 years. I had four boys and two girls. My world back then was all about children. I did not work outside my home. I watched other people's children. I also taught music to the children at Sunday School. I felt safe with little ones. They rarely judged me and seldom made me feel inferior. I rarely felt comfortable around adults. I always felt inferior during conversations unless they were about children. If the Lord thought I should go back to school, then I wanted to have an occupation revolving around children. Unfortunately, that was not to be the case. Any government program that would fund my education, would do so for only two years. I tossed out the idea of grade-school teacher and replaced it with that of becoming a Registered Nurse.

Of course, this added more pain as my peers and classmates for the most part were younger, prettier, and just out of high school. It is fair to say, that in the beginning, I stayed to myself.

I did not join in conversations and prayed that I would not be called upon to answer any questions in class. I was so very shy and had only God to talk to about my insecurities. Things soon changed however, when we had to participate in the Nursing lab and go to clinicals in various hospitals.

My nursing instructor and first year advisor, recognized my plight when the hospital staff found me on the floor of my first patient's room. My patient could not put on his call light as he saw my knees buckle, sending me to the cold hospital floor. He was suffering from a stroke. I was suffering from a profound case of anxiety, worried that he would choke to death when I fed him. When he choked on a tiny bite of food, I choked too. Great nurse I'd be. They would be calling a code "blue" on me if I didn't shape up! Instructor Mary made sure I had a chair to sit on as I watched my first C-section. One of those little round doctor's stools didn't prevent me from hitting the floor a second time. Giving my first shot was entertaining too. Good thing I told my patient to roll to her side. She never saw how many times my shaking hypodermic almost entered her toosh before I finally got up enough nerve to stick it to her. Of course, I had to have a lab partner with a deviated septum. I was the only one who could not get a nasogastric tube down their lab partner.

My self- esteem just plummeted. Mary and I had many after class discussions. She was always positive. She had unlimited faith in me. I think Mary was one of those promised angels. She found scholarship after scholarship to help pay my cost of textbooks and childcare. I had no problem with studies and grades, but I thought I would never feel comfortable in the lab or hospital setting. Then one day I had to role play actual hospital emergencies in our nursing lab. I felt comfortable with drama. My entire life had been one continuous soap opera. I received stupendous applause as I became a "ready to deliver" patient on our gurney. Lucille Ball would have been proud.

For the first time, I felt at ease, just like being at home with my little ones. Then one day in Anatomy and Physiology class, our instructor asked for a volunteer to verbally trace the vessels that a drop of blood would have to go through to get from one part of the body to another. No one would volunteer, and I had no plans to either. Those nasty little lips of mine were talking to themselves and before you know it the instructor asked them to speak a little bit louder. The class cheered her on.

To my amazement and everyone else's, that drop of blood found its way to its destination without backtracking once. It didn't take long before I was willingly volunteering in class. Before the end of the semester, I was asked to join in at lunch. People soon knew I was the mother of six. People soon knew that my Heavenly Father was a real part of my life. Everyone came to know that I was very poor, but never poor in spirit. Each memory of failure was soon replaced with success.

It did not matter that I had dropped out of high school. The memories of success were lessening those of defeat. It took a tremendous amount of study. I promised the Lord I would keep His day special and did not study on the Sabbath, and He made up the difference for the lost day studying. I paid my tithing, my one tenth to the Lord. Sixty dollars was a lot of money for me. I felt it was such a small offering to give. He knew it was everything. He opened the windows of Heaven and gave us blessings that others would call mere coincidences. For me they were His way of letting me know He was right there. I watched myself evolve from a frightened young mother into a confident mother and graduate nurse.

Before long, I held my first job as a Registered Nurse. Soon, I was the team leader. When I had the assignment as Charge Nurse, I think back to those moments when panic was in charge, and I found myself on the floor.

I now precept nursing students. I watch their hands shake as they place their first IV. Mine are now quick and steady. Never would I have thought I was successful, except as a mother. That for sure, has been my most important calling. My children were there to watch all the struggles. They were also there as we knelt in prayer to thank God for what we had, and to ask Him for what we needed. We learned the difference between our wants and our needs. As each child grew, I was pleased to see their ability to give and share, especially with those less fortunate. They have also seen how Heavenly Father answered our prayers. We would pray for shoes and we would soon hear of a program giving a pair of shoes away. When we were low on food, someone would always bring extra by. When our house needed repair, the people in the church would help us willingly.

I came to know my Father in Heaven as my closest friend. He knew the person I had the power to be. Long before nursing school, He gave me the gifts of organization and compassion. He knew I would need them. Those three long years were difficult. I never thought for a moment they wouldn't be. But I knew with every fiber of my being that He was always there. I could never imagine him sending me six sweet children without helping me find a way to raise and care for them. I look back at the close friends I had during nursing school and know they were sent my way. I know that during difficult times, angels were watching over us. No harm or accident came our way during that time. As the years passed by, I was able to pass on the love and the hope Father in Heaven gave to me. We had nothing worldly back then, but we had everything because we had hope. We were rich in the things that mattered because we always had faith enough to know He was there.

Anatomy and Physiology 101: The body has a pressure-release valve. It can be activated by placing the body in a kneeling position, with both arms folded and both eyes closed. (Start praying.)

Tests, Tests and More Tests!

I am not a test taker. I never was. I think my Dad gave me those genes. Thank you so much. Let us tell you what we have learned, and we'll do just fine. Have us prove it on paper and fear takes over. Now, to make things worse, as every nursing student knows, or will soon find out, nursing exam questions usually have more than one correct answer. That is how the final nursing exam is presented. It is all multiple choice. Now you would think a test like that can't possibly be that difficult. Well, there you go thinking, and keep right on thinking until you have the most correct answer. Is it A, C and E? Is it only A and C? Is it all the above? Or is it none of the above? Now to make matters worse, many of the questions will lead you down a path that will start you thinking in the wrong direction.

We were all warned about that right from the beginning. We were being prepared for the Nursing Boards we were to take two years down the road. We were all being taught to use judgment decisions and being prepared to *think like nurses*. Back in the early eighties, there were too many nurses in the field. Students were accepted into nursing programs knowing that one third of their classmates would never make it to graduation. We were the instructor's garden of little hopefuls. If you could not bloom in the proper way, they would simply PLUCK YOU OUT!

It was on a crisp, fall morning that I entered the classroom to take my first nursing exam. I felt great. I was calm. Anyone would know it. Just look at my sweaty palms. Listen to that churning stomach, and please ignore the tapping of my feet!

"Remember students, all books on the floor. You may ask an instructor if you don't understand the question. (Oh, that calms the soul) You have one hour and please, remember you are looking for the most correct answer." (No pressure there).

With the clock ticking ever so loudly, I began. What a trap! They gave us two easy questions just to make us think we really knew something. Or was that too easy? I'd better look the first two over again. Wasn't that what they were really asking, I wondered. I'll just put a question mark here on the side, so I can go back to it. Fifteen minutes had gone by. There were 50 questions. I had answered 12. Six of the questions had question marks beside them. Pick up your pace, Kim! Anxiety was taking over. The clock ticked loudly, much too loudly. I felt like I was headed for the guillotine. This test was murder! Just kill me now and then I won't have to take more of these tests. I was losing the battle. I was so anxious, I started feeling waves of nausea. Then old Satan took a stab.

"You're not that smart. What were you ever thinking? You don't have what it takes to become a nurse."

I had felt those feelings before. Suddenly my thoughts went back to The Dalles, Oregon.

"What happens to you and your little ones will be in your hands. This is up to you. Heavenly Father wants you to succeed."

I closed my eyes and though I could not kneel, my prayer was from the heart.

"Help me, Father. If a nurse is what you know I can become, then, help me pass this test!"

A reassuring calm encompassed me. I took some deep breaths. "Turn the test over," I was prompted. "Start at the end. Mark the first answer that comes to your mind. Do not change it." I did so quickly and carefully. Do not doubt yourself, I commanded. You can do this, my thoughts insisted. Father in Heaven will help you.

"Time is up! All pencils down, please."

I was spent, emotionally and physically. I wondered for two long days, what my fate was to be. Then during our next nursing class, our tests were returned. I was never as thankful to receive a "B." On that day, a "B" meant everything to me. Soon the B's would turn into A's. That first test taught me a valuable lesson. Your first response to a test question is usually correct. Most times when you change an answer, you will be changing it to the wrong answer. Never again did I begin a test with doubts about who I was or what I could become. That first test was passed with help from a kind Heavenly Father. For future tests, He was going to bless me with reinforcements

— a most wonderful circle of friends.

A Circle of Friends

Making the transition from wife and mother to single parent and student was extremely difficult for me. My world before divorce had always revolved around church friends and children. I loved motherhood and felt very comfortable around little ones. I was the children's chorister for my church for many years. Children did not intimidate me. Children don't judge people the way adults do. They accept you for who you are.

When I went through divorce, two major changes took place in my life. I lost my close circle of married friends and I was forced for the first time to interact with strangers. This dilemma was further complicated by the fact that I was sensitive and extremely shy. I felt at a loss to know who "me" really was back then. As I walked through the college doorways, its cafeteria and classrooms, I felt lonely and often inferior to the young girls that I saw there. I felt like my life was all "backwards," going forward, but certainly in the wrong order, like an incorrectly spliced video. There I was at age 30, the mother of six, tackling the milestones of those who were in their twenties. I usually rushed into the cafeteria to eat my lunch and quickly retreated to the library to study. I would rather be alone than risk more failure.

On one November day, all was about to change. The only empty seat I could find in the cafeteria was across from a lady who appeared to be in her forties. She struck up a conversation (and I came to know she always would) and before long we were really enjoying each other's company. Her name was Evette.

Before long, a single lady our age, Anna, joined us as seats became empty. Mariah soon greeted Evette and then we were four. Mariah waved to signal Liz and I could tell their lunch circle was complete. I was introduced to everyone by Evette.

Evette, like me, was newly divorced after many years of marriage. Mariah and Liz were married. Except for Anna, we all had families. Earlier, in September, we had all entered the Nursing Program. Each of us was equally stressed with this new change in our lives. I guess today it would really seem simple, but back then, I was so pleased that I could fit into an adult conversation for the space of an hour.

When lunch ended and we separated to go different directions, they all said they would see each other the same time and same place the next day. What changed my life for the next two years was that I was invited to join. Those four women would become my dearest and closest friends. We would study together for hours on end. We practiced on one another when it came time to start our first IV's. We discovered that Evette had a deviated septum when we couldn't get an NG tube to slide down her throat. We practiced bed making until all sheet corners were perfectly tucked in and gave bed baths until we were squeaky clean.

We shared our successes and could confess our failures to one another. When they saw that I had only two outfits for my daily attire, they planned a wonderful birthday party with beautiful gifts that helped me feel fit for any occasion. Once a month on a Saturday afternoon, we made meals to stick in our freezers for hard study days. Two of us would quiz the three who were chosen to be the day's chefs.

The thing that I will always remember most and always cherish, was the love that we shared for our Heavenly Father. You see, we all had a belief in God even though each one of us practiced a different religion. We soon became known as the group that would succeed on our tests. Our scores were high, and our spirits soared because we faced each test together. We studied for all major tests *together*. But before we took up pen or pencil, we did something that no other study group did before entering the testing room. We prayed. We formed a circle. We joined our hands, and we petitioned our Father in Heaven to help us know the right answers. Not only did we pray that our efforts would produce correct answers, but we asked Him to guide us each week to the most important information we needed to focus our studies on. Just before we entered the door, we invited anyone who wanted to, to join our circle of prayer. We did not back away into a private room, but instead stood just outside the door. We thanked Him for our friendships and our struggles, our joys and our sorrows and asked Him to let each test take us one step closer to accomplishing our dream, that of becoming a Registered Nurse.

The "Buddy" System

Thank heavens for the Head Start Program. It was a God-send and a blessing for our family. As I started the Nursing program at Portland Community College, I did so as a single parent. Four of those children were in school and the youngest two were not. Bjarne and Buddy were three and five. I will never forget their first day there. Thank goodness they had one another.

Little B.J., as we called him, was afraid of everything and that day was no exception. His tiny hand dug into mine as I had to leave him there for his first day. I was crying and so was he.

His teacher saw our plight and gently said, "This first time will be the hardest. It will be o.k."

The first day was the most difficult. Those first few days were heart-wrenching for us all. B.J., however, hid under a table for almost six weeks upon arrival to the Head Start

Center, but by Christmas time he saw Head Start as an adventure and he loved his teachers.

One morning, and of course, it had to be the morning of an important test, my alarm clock did not go off and we all overslept. I was frazzled and rushed. I knew this was not a good example to set for my first test day. Socks were flying, and kids were wailing as they all had to share our one bathroom and in such a short space of time. With nearly 200 teeth brushed and backpacks in hand, we all piled into the "Blue Bomb" and raced the two miles to Head Start. With any luck, I would have just enough time after dropping off the older ones to make it to the college.

The car door opened and B.J. presented himself. I peered into the back of the car when Buddy did not follow.

"Come on now, Buddy, you need to hurry, or we will all be late!"

"Where is Buddy?" "I didn't wake him up!" " I didn't either."

It was unanimous. No one woke Buddy up.

"Mama, I don't think he's here," said seven-year-old Kari, as she started to cry.

I was the one who wanted to cry.

I was so worried about my test, but I was beyond frantic knowing that I had left my small child at home alone. Boy could that ugly "Blue Bomb" go, and it could stop just as fast, right at our front door. We were all so worried we would find him crying from the stress of being left behind. How we all laughed when we found Buddy. Oblivious to his family's torment and sleeping like a baby, he was tucked up soundly in his own little bed.

It is amazing how fast our Buddy got ready for school that day. With five siblings grabbing his backpack, shoes and clothes, the only thing he had to do for himself was chew his food and hit the bathroom. Did I make it to my test on time? Of course not! Did I get a lecture? To be sure! My instructor, however, thought my story was so funny that it had to be true, so she arranged for another test time.

This mother of six learned a valuable lesson. We started a new system the very next day and named it after its rightful originator, "The Budster." An older child always looked out for one younger, and no one was ever left behind again. Maybe I should learn to count to six before taking Algebra 500. Do you think?

Rich in the Things That Matter

I would be remiss if my book did not include a chapter about Juanita, for it was this sweet friend that taught me the lessons of love and compassion. She became the conduit and means by which Heavenly Father could pour out his riches blessings upon my family during the bleakest time of my life. I hope someday that her fingers might turn these pages, that she might understand my gratitude and just what she meant to me, for I do not think she ever really knew.

Juanita was a member of my church congregation years ago in the late 70s. She was the newly divorced mother of five young children. I was the married mother of six young children. My marriage was less than wonderful. What I realize now, but did not then, was that Juanita was extremely lonely. She would call me frequently, often several times a day, though I did not have enough time to talk for minutes on end. In a strange way, I felt that her poor misfortune of being alone and divorced might somehow fall upon my head.

I did not know Juanita well at that time. I did know that she was a gifted seamstress. She was at every baby shower, graciously giving a hand-made quilt or baby bunting to each expectant mother. If she was unhappy, she did not let it show. She cheerfully mingled among the guests and was never void of conversation. I did know that Juanita felt inadequate, being a member of a church that cherished families and mates being together forever. I later learned that she was intent on never settling for anything less than a virtuous and splendid man to raise her little family. She prayed often that she would not succumb to immorality and that Heavenly Father would give her the strength to do so. I watched her as she sifted out the occasional male suitor, telling him to keep at bay. I did not know how Juanita could raise such a family of little ones alone. I was content not to ask. As I think back then, I did not really want to know. It was enough to consider my own struggles at that time, for even though I was poor, I was still married. I did not know it then, but that comfort was soon to change.

It was in January of 1982 that I found myself to be the newly divorced mother of six little children. Before long, I was the one to find myself lonely, living in a strange town and longing for home. I was not able to return to Portland, Oregon until the spring of that year. I was thrilled to move closer to my family, but divorce in Portland was just as lonely as divorce in The Dalles. I was struggling not only with depression, but also with the reality that we were destitute, living on a monthly check of $610.00.

Six hundred and ten dollars was my monthly income for housing and utilities, clothes and non-food items like soap, shampoo and toilet paper, and all the necessary items that food stamps could not buy. I had no idea how we were ever going to make it. I did not even know how to start. Heavenly Father did though. He was aware of my struggling little family. He could see that I was short on hope. He was so kind. Perhaps I could have found out about how God helps His poor, with a great deal of researching and phone calls, but instead he sent me the love of Juanita.

I did not deserve her phone call, and I certainly was not worthy of her friendship. She however, thought I was. She had walked in the shoes I was about to slip on. She knew the best paths those shoes should travel, for she—bless her soul—had broken a trail that would give us hope. Little did I know, as I started down this path, that it would bring me closer to my

Savior in a way I had never experienced before. I came to know that He knew my every need, great and small. It was my responsibility to ask and to have the faith I needed. It was His promise to never leave me alone. I came to know, in the most literal ways, what it means to have prayers answered.

Juanita called me every day. She knew when there was gleaning. What fun we had picking pears and peaches and apples with all 11 children. No sooner would I tell Heavenly Father that we had no winter coats, then a phone call would come from Juanita telling me of a program having gently-used coats for free. Shoes were always an expensive need, but Juanita found program after program that kept my children in shoes through my three years of nursing school.

This was a humbling time, for people would give me their hand-me-downs and sometimes they were not always kind. One afternoon I looked at my boys' jeans (more patches than jeans) and asked for Heavenly Father's help in prayer that night. The next morning a neighbor lady came to my door with two bags of jeans, wondering if my "little rag muffins" could use them as she noticed how torn theirs were because my youngest boys played with her son. Biting my tongue, and ignoring her jibes, I accepted them kindly, though it was not kindness I was feeling at that moment.

Opportunities to help us survive did not always present themselves at the best moments. One time I found my living room filled with boxes of fresh corn. My studies could not wait, but neither could the corn. Two hundred pints soon filled our shelves and lasted until graduation. We remained incredibly poor during those three long years; however, we were never poor in spirit. My children joined in the circle with folded arms as we asked Heavenly Father to help us have those things we really needed. They were also there as they saw prayers answered in mysterious ways. My youngest son has often told me how amazing these events were to him and how he too realized that such experiences could not be justified as mere coincidences.

Juanita married a wonderful man from Fiji and added many

beautiful children to her family. Much of the material she had tucked away in her "material room" was made into beautiful dresses and shirts for her children. Juanita taught me the value of love. She taught me the value of friendship. Heavenly Father was to let me return only a small portion of her thoughtfulness in an astonishing way.

Juanita called me one day to tell me she was being treated for a sore lump in her breast. She said her doctor told her it was mastitis from a plugged duct from breast feeding her littlest child. She had been on a course of antibiotics and the soreness was not improving. Her doctor reassured her, "it would just take time." She felt frustrated and worried. Two weeks later there had been no change. I felt an urgent prompting to tell her to get a second opinion. Worried about the money it might cost, having several little children and one on the way, she continued to hesitate. It was then that I suggested her husband give her a blessing to know what to do. Her husband gave her a blessing which told her to seek medical help quickly. Juanita was wheeled to surgery the day after her visit with a second doctor. She had cancer and it was growing rapidly because of the hormones that her body was producing due to her pregnancy. Juanita would have lost her life had it not been for her surgery. She refused to terminate her pregnancy to start chemotherapy and a few months later delivered a beautiful and healthy little son.

I have thought of Juanita often. I sometimes reflect on those most difficult times. My testimony of the Gospel was based on the things that I read and pondered, a logical testimony, you might say. I am profoundly grateful for the opportunity I was allowed to exercise my faith.

I am certain that Juanita never imagined that she would add several more beautiful children and have the blessing to remarry again. I would never have thought that after bringing six little ones into this world that they would have their lives shattered by divorce. I came to have greater faith. Juanita was the first person to help me understand about trials and tribulations. The trial you face does not really matter. The way you go through the trial has all the significance in the world. You learn nothing if your heart is hardened with each test. You will soon find yourself bitter. If you face each trial having faith that it has purpose, your testimony will no longer just be a logical one. You will come to know your loving and kind Heavenly Father in a profoundly intimate way. I testify to you that He is there as we take that first breath and our parents hear our first cry. He is there along each path we choose, even if our choices take us along trails that get us lost for a while. And He is certainly there to welcome us back into his arms when our journey is finished. Our spiritual gifts will be ours forever. When we come to understand this, we will we be rich in the things that matter.

Please Help Us Find A New Home

There have been times in my life, just as I am sure there have been times in yours, when you wonder why bad things happen to good people. Times like those can test us to our core and place our faith in Heavenly Father on trial. Such was the case for me and my little family back in 1983.

I believe it was in the spring. My youngest was four, my oldest 13. I was just finishing my first year of nursing school. We were living in Portland. I had recently been accepted in the Section 8 housing program in Clackamas County. We were excited and had been looking diligently for a new place to live, one closer to my sister and to my school. We found that our task was going to be difficult because many landlords were not willing to rent to a single parent with six children, especially on the Section 8 program.

It was during this time that I met a man at one of our

church dances. He was not a church member. I had gone out with him a couple of times and one Saturday, I asked him to join my family for swimming at the YMCA and dinner at our house. I thought it was strange how he gravitated towards my two little girls and wanted to toss them in the water with no thought towards my sons. I'm sure the Holy Ghost was trying to warn me, even then. As the afternoon progressed, I wanted to end the date but couldn't think of a way to do so. The uncomfortable feeling continued to linger. My oldest was going to his friend's house for the evening and with my kids tucked in and the house all quiet, I just wanted my date to say goodnight.

My night turned into terror when he forcefully and with extreme anger assaulted me. I did not dare cry out for help, as I was afraid what he might do to my children. Crying and hurt, I was able to convince him to leave, but not before he burst into tears. It became clear how emotionally unstable he really was. He lived about 50 miles away, but I was so frightened I stayed awake all night, fearing that he did not drive home.

The next day, he was there, pounding on our door. My kids became frightened when I would not let them answer. I was afraid to leave my house and afraid to go anywhere without all my children by my side. Later that evening, I knelt quietly in my bedroom and talked with my Father. I told Him how frightened I was. I asked him if there was another house for us. I was precise in what I asked for, even though I suspected he already knew. We needed a house with four bedrooms to meet the housing standards. The rent could be no more than $350.00 a month, and if it were at all possible, we needed to be closer to my sister Eileen. I was on my knees for what seemed like hours, and then, tired and depressed, I climbed into bed.

The next morning, I safely delivered my little ones to their respective schools. I was anxious and felt sick to my stomach from so much stress and elected to go visit my sister and take more time to pray that day. I called Eileen and asked if I could come see her at lunch. I remember how she thought it was unlike me to miss a day of classes. I was tired, anxious and I am sure that my mind must have been wandering when I missed the road that led to her house. I then had to go another way. I was less than a mile from her home when I noticed a large sign attached to a telephone pole. It read "House For Rent." I followed the sign's arrow and searched out the printed address. Hm, I thought. There was a cute, little green home that rested on an enormous lot. What happened from that moment on became orchestrated by this world's most praised Conductor.

I walked up to the house and knocked on the door. I was greeted by a young couple who quickly invited me in. The living room was full of boxes stacked halfway to the ceiling. The couple was preparing to leave the next morning. My hopes were dashed when they said they knew the house had already been rented. At this point, most people would walk away with a "Thank You." I did not. I felt prompted to ask to look through the house. Most people wouldn't welcome the intrusion with it already being rented, but the young couple did not mind at all. Two loft bedrooms were upstairs. Two bedrooms were downstairs. One was large. One was tiny with no closet and only room for a bed and dresser. The kitchen was big and cheerful, with windows looking out over the backyard, an enormous backyard. The living room was big and the only bathroom was small.

"This could work," I told myself.

I couldn't believe that I asked them for the landlord's phone number. It was even a bigger surprise that I found myself using their phone to call their landlord (a bank manager) at work. What aggressive spirit had taken over the reserved and shy Kim?

My hopes were dashed once more when she said, "It has already been rented. The man is coming to sign papers tonight!" She was not happy to be contacted at her place of employment.

I just would not let myself be told no, and I simply did not understand why. My dad was even more surprised when he got a call from me that afternoon. I never called him at work.

Never! I asked him to meet me there at that little house that evening. Why I wanted him to go was a question I could not answer. All I knew was that he was supposed to be there. Dad decided to go along with his newly crazed daughter and loyally met me there at the same time the landlord said she would be meeting the new renter.

We saw a beautiful black Lincoln pull up into that little house's driveway. I was sure it was Jan, the landlord. Almost an hour passed by, but no one else arrived. My dad was so patient. Then Jan said good-bye to the young couple and started to leave. If the new renter was already inside or had walked there earlier before we had arrived, what I did next could have made me look like such a fool.

I took my chance and leaped (no, flew!) out of my car.

"You must be Jan," I panted. "I am Kim. I talked with you earlier today about your house."

"I just don't understand," she said. "I was sure he wanted the house, but I just called him, and he has changed his mind." She was tired and irritated, but I motioned for my Dad and she invited us both back inside.

"Six children?" she asked. "Where would you put them?"

So, I showed her.

"And "Section 8? Oh," she paused. "I'm just not sure, and the basement, it leaks when it rains hard." She tried her hardest to discourage us from renting.

It then became crystal clear why I asked my dad to come along. "You will never have to worry about getting your rent on time with Section 8," said my dad, "and my daughter keeps a house as neat as a pin! Now, as for that basement, I'm a concrete foreman by trade and do I have a deal for you! I can fix that leaking basement for free if you will rent to my daughter."

Do miracles happen? Of course, they do. A wrong turn on the road led me to the right turn in my life. Coincidence? I believe not.

Let's see now. I found you just the right house. You will be on Section 8. It has four bedrooms and rents for $350.00. And by the way, you can

walk to visit Eileen. So glad we had this conversation. Call me at home, anytime. I miss you too.
Heavenly Father

My Greatest Nursing Mentor

I remember my greatest nursing mentor. Her name was Mary Blake. She was my first-year advisor at Portland Community College. I was newly divorced and suddenly a single mother of six, five under the age of nine. Mary became my friend, a most compassionate friend. Could she ever understand what her words meant to a lonely and frightened high school drop out?

"Kim, you must do this." Kim, you can do this." "Kim, others are watching."

Mary was there to watch me pass out and tumble to the floor with my first patient. I was so nervous about feeding a man on choking precautions that I toppled over from fear. That day Mary taught me the importance of eating something before I saw my patients.

When I could not afford my own textbooks, Mary secretly submitted my name for the Portland Business Women's Scholarship. She taught me that children won't die if you occasionally feed them Cheerios for dinner. Still, Mary knew that I needed to keep my pride intact, so she quietly took up a fund to replace my only outfit—a sad pair of black slacks and a brown plaid shirt—then made sure to anonymously give it to me on my birthday so I would be a graceful recipient.

Mary radiated a love that never ceased. She did not let me know until the TV cameras were in place that I had been chose to receive the Dr. DeBernardis Scholarship. Mary knew I was prone to fainting! It was Mary who pinned me on graduation day.

I was so nervous, and she whispered in my ear, "Oh Kim, your family must be so proud."

And it was true. My children's voices could be heard above all others.

Mary, do you know that my three-year-old is now 21? I have you to thank for all that I have accomplished, for all that I have become. And Mary, you were right. Others were watching.

SPECIAL NOTE: I wrote this story in honor of Mary during Nurses' Week in 2001. When I found out it was to be published, I tried to locate Mary so that she might know. I could find no leads as to her whereabouts. I decided to ask for some divine intervention and petitioned Father in Heaven to help me find her. Once again, He lovingly answered my prayer. It was during that same week that I had a patient most eager to go home. Her taxi was waiting. Our nurse's aide was too busy to take my patient to the hospital's main entrance. I chose to help her out. I got my patient settled into the car and accidentally bumped into an older lady as I turned the wheelchair around. I recognized Mary immediately. After 16 years, she remembered my name, and along with so many other sweet words of encouragement in the past, she added to them that day.

"Kim, how could I ever forget you?"

In Honor of Mary

Others Were Watching

My career as a student nurse was coming to an end. It was only two weeks before finals. Line upon line, precept upon precept, I had mastered the cardiac system, the respiratory system and all those systems I would need knowledge of to become a nurse. My nervous system however was about to short circuit. My anxiety level had long since passed ten on the one-to-ten scale. I could not fall into a restful sleep one night after another. I was becoming irritable with my children. Katie who was now 11 continued to demonstrate the pure faith of a child.

"Mama," she comforted, "you need a blessing."

"Oh, I just can't," I said to myself.

Patriarch Hall had done so much for me and my little family. He and Sister Hall had appointed themselves as our "Home Teachers" for three long years.* They had known me as a teenager. They had watched me bring one little one after another into this world, only to see my life fall apart with divorce. They were there at every turn.

The "Blue Bomb," as we affectionately called our car, belched her last breath and died. Even Katie's prayers could not resurrect her one last time. Patriarch Hall loaned us his Honda until I could graduate and qualify for a new loan. Kind favors and blessings of comfort were, at times, the glue that held my family together. The Halls never made me feel like I was a burden to them. They were gracious and caring. They were always kind.

I explained my situation to Patriarch Hall as he and his sweet companion arrived at my home that evening. I remember that night so clearly. I remember the touch of his hands upon my head. They felt steady and warm.

He began my blessing by pronouncing my given name and then he paused. I knew the Spirit of the Holy Ghost was there, allowing Patriarch Hall's hands to become the channel through which Heavenly Father's council could be conveyed. His words pierced my heart and would never be forgotten. He told me how angels had been watching over me and my family, and how the Lord had placed them there. They were there to give me strength. to help me proceed with courage.

"You cannot quit. You must stay strong!" he stated. "Kim,

the reasons are far more reaching than the needs of your family and their future. In due time you will come to know them." I was blessed with peace and strength and I knew that those promises were mine to keep.

Did I pass all of those exams? Yes, and with angels near my side. That, however, a miracle by itself, was not the miracle Patriarch Hall spoke of. I worked my first five years as a nurse with a registry so that I might always be home near to the time my kids came home from school. During those first six months I worked in 12 different hospitals around the Portland metropolitan area. That is when my blessing began to be fulfilled. The first little revelation seemed like simple coincidence and only that. Just before leaving work another nurse came up to me.

"Are you Kim?" she questioned. "My sister was in your nursing class. She left the nursing program just long enough to have her twins. She told me about you. She said you have six children. She said she had to finish and would not drop out because of two children when you had six."

The next time was at a different hospital. Throughout that day I worked on a floor with a nurse that seemed quite familiar to me. She removed all doubt when she told me we were in the same graduating class. She had gone through a painful divorce during that time. She shared her story.

"I was so close to quitting that final semester. I was so depressed. The group of students I studied with told me that you were going to school because of your divorce. I never knew you had so many children. It was the kick in the toosh I needed."

Then there was the young man at the grocery store. He overheard the checker ask me how I liked being a nurse instead of a nursing student. He also caught my name. Once again, a story unfolded.

His wife was in my class. They were overwhelmed with debt and had lost their home. They had to make the choice of having her go back to work or finish the nursing program. I remembered her. I spoke with her after a class one afternoon. I told her that my poverty was only a temporary situation. Staying in school would make it possible for me to someday take care of my family. Quitting school to take a low paying job would always keep me struggling. He asked if he could offer a hug. I received it graciously.

I soon started counting these reoccurring revelations. They soon totaled six. Only my Father in Heaven knew how important it was for me to remain strong. He placed angels round about me to give me added strength the evening of my blessing. This strength was not just for me, for only Father knew, "Others were watching."

**Patriarch* is a special office in my church. We also call each other *brother* and *sister*. *Home teachers* are usually two people assigned to a family to help them out spiritually and temporally.

3 A TREE STANDING TALL IN THE WIND (LOSING THE ONES WE LOVE)

Winds will come, and storms may rage, but dear Father,
if your arms are wrapped tightly around me, I cannot be uprooted.

    I have heard the cries of a young mother, pleading with me to bring her stillborn back to life. I have held the hand of my sweet father as he took his last labored breath. I have witnessed the anguish of my own daughter as she kissed her newborn son goodbye and I have stood next to my son's father as the white sheet was removed from our son's face at the morgue.

    At times, I did not think I could bear their pain or that of my own. There were times I did not want to wake for the day, knowing that it was not a dream, knowing that my loved one was indeed gone. Heavenly Father was there for me each day, helping me and helping my loved ones to heal. As time pressed forward, day by day, the heaviness of my broken heart lightened, and I began to heal. I had no way of knowing that the pain and despair of it all would one day and on many days help others remain rooted as they went through intense sorrow and storms of their own.

I Am Not So Far Away

On the morning of March 28th, 1987, my alarm clock woke me from a deep and peaceful sleep. It took a moment for me to feel oriented, and I soon remembered that it was my weekend off. It was 4:50 a.m. on Saturday morning and I did not have to go into work. The ringing of the alarm seemed odd to me because my clock was always set for 5:15 a.m. on the days that I worked. It was not set that morning and certainly not for the time it rang. I could not fall back to sleep.

A piercing uneasiness started to overtake me. It was almost like having a panic attack, except in this case there was nothing that I was worried about. The feeling would not leave me. I got up and out of bed and quietly walked around our little duplex, careful not to disturb sleeping children. I opened the living room door to see fog hovering in all the stillness and was unable to see the nearby road. I felt an unsettling apprehension, an eeriness almost. Where was this anxiety centered? What was its source?" It was so powerful that I could not sit; I could not focus.

When the morning sun began to push through the fog, I grabbed a shovel and started preparing a little flower bed for petunias that I was going to plant later that day. Even as my children awakened one by one, I continued to feel uneasy. They sensed my quietness and asked if I was all right. I wasn't. I had never in my life felt this way. I felt an impending doom but could not explain why.

I had been struggling for hours when the phone rang. It was my oldest brother. He had just received a phone call from the Clackamas County Police. There had been an accident. They had been trying for hours to locate the parents of Tony

Knudson, my oldest son. They would give no information over the phone. My brother had given them my new address and I knew the news could not be good.

Tony was just 17. He had emancipated himself and recently moved to his own apartment with a group of friends. I can still see so vividly in my mind, now, many years later, those moments when the police arrived. Remembering that time still hits the center of my core and fills my eyes with tears. Telling me that there was an accident, that there were fatalities did not help me to understand what no mother ever wants to hear. Their words were garbled, distant.

"I don't understand," I said.

"Your son died early this morning, Ms. Knudson. In a car accident," they said softy.

Tony had missed a turn on the slippery pavement, going over the maximum speed of the curve that foggy, damp morning. His tire caught the guide wire to a power pole as his car spun out of control. It hit with great force as it wrapped around the pole, ejecting Tony and his best friend Robert out of the sprung back hatch. They died instantly. The friend that they had dropped off minutes before was alive to tell the officers the events of that evening. I fell to the ground as I heard the news. Nothing could console me as the officers carried me into my home.

The next few days became clear, as my grief was unbearable. My son had passed away sometime between 4:45 and 5:00 a.m. that morning. I did not receive the news until one o'clock in the afternoon. I have often wondered if my son had been in my room right after his death and if he was trying to say goodbye before he left this world.

I know to this day that I have always regretted what happened the evening before. As I left the parking lot of the gas station where he worked, I felt overwhelmingly prompted to return and give my tall and handsome 17-year-old a hug, just to let him know how much I loved him. But I was concerned about embarrassing him at work and did not go back. Holding my son's still and broken body in my arms at the mortuary I rocked him and cried until I could bear it no longer, then released him to the caretakers. That was to be the last hug I would ever give my son.

Spot

My elderly neighbor and good friend Bill had watched from his window as the police officers had given me the news about Tony that March afternoon. This sweet man waited until later that day to offer his sympathy, out of respect, and because he simply did not know how to tell me that there was more bad news to share. Tears were streaming down my cheeks when I opened my door for him. His strong and loving arms enfolded me as he shared my sorrow.

He told me that I needed to go see my neighbor who lived on the left of me. She had something to tell me. It was important. He offered to go along. I never could remember her first name. What I could remember is how she loved my children and their pets. She was always asking the kids to come in for a little treat.

Bill knocked on her door for me that afternoon. She could see I had been crying, and tears welled up in her eyes as she started to tell her story. She told me that early that morning, about 4:45 a.m., she kept hearing a cat meow outside her bedroom window. At first, she thought her big tom cat was after a cat in the neighborhood. As she began to awaken, she realized that the cries, were piercing, hurt cries, so she went to her front door. There near the door at the top of her porch was Tony's cat, Spot. Spot had been living at our house because Tony could not have her in his new apartment. She had been my gift to Tony when he was just a little boy. When she turned the porch light on, she could see instantly that Spot had most likely been hit by a car. Her beautiful calico fur was covered in blood. She was trembling, so my neighbor placed a soft towel around Spot as she picked her up. Spot died in her arms. She excused herself from the room for a moment and then returned with a box.

As she handed me Tony's cherished Spot, I asked. "What time did Spot pass away?"

"It was just a few minutes before five o'clock," she said. "Please, don't think I'm a crazy old lady, I just don't think Tony could leave this world without her."

I did not think she was crazy at all.

A Letter from Tony

Working as a nurse, I have come to know the many faces of death. Sometimes it comes slowly, allowing the family to put all affairs in order, and say their final good-byes. Sometimes death comes quickly, not giving loved ones enough time to grieve and to prepare for the feeling of loss. And then there are times, with no warning at all, it comes and the opportunity to say farewell is gone forever. Those times are the most difficult, I believe. Or at least, it was so for me.

On the day of my son's passing, I learned just how frail life can be. It also made me acutely aware that life can end without notice. It can end without having a chance to say goodbye. I came to the realization on the day of my son's death that what we have become and how we have treated others here in this life are by far more important than any earthly possession we will leave behind.

By the time the police were able to notify me of my son's fate that morning, Tony's apartment had been pilfered. Tony and his best friend Robert died together that morning. Well-meaning friends had taken most of these two young men's possessions as mementos to remember them by. The remains of their apartment did not even have enough so that each of Tony's five siblings could keep a small remembrance of their older brother. My father quickly obtained all the papers remaining in the apartment, so that we might settle Tony's earthly affairs. With my son's funeral arrangements to make and five younger children to comfort, I put the four sacks of papers aside.

The next two days were intense. Each night I would drift off to sleep, only to reawaken with the realization that my son was gone. It was not a dream. Reflecting over my son's short life left me even more saddened. Tony had struggled much of his teenage years with many of the decisions he was making. Peer pressure and his youth often pushed him down pathways that he knew were not right. Although my son knew I loved him, he made many choices, such as running away, that would keep us from loving and meaningful conversations. He had prematurely moved out on his own, creating an emotional distance between us that I could not shorten. His untimely death would make that permanent. How I longed to talk to him. I had so much I wanted to say.

Hundreds of young people attended my son's funeral. The most important one that day would be a man that came up to me afterwards whose name I never learned. I have often wondered if he was real. Many times, I have thought he was a messenger from Heavenly Father on behalf of my son. When I shook this man's hand, he seemed truly kind.

"You must be Tony's mother," he said. "Tony has talked about you often. He has written many letters to you. I know how much he loved you." I never saw the man again.

I thought it was strange that he mentioned letters. How would he know that? Tony was an extremely private person. I had never received a letter from my son. We lived only a few miles apart, so we did not keep in touch through letters.

The day after my son's funeral, I kept thinking about that conversation and decided to go through those four sacks of papers. I sorted through bills and receipts, and by the time I had gone through the third sack, there were no personal letters to be found. I was sorting through the final sack and there at the bottom, folded over several times, was a letter.

The handwriting was Tony's. The letter started, "Dear Mom." I slowly and carefully read each word as his thoughts unfolded. In his letter he thanked me for giving him the gift of life and choosing not to have an abortion. He expressed his gratitude for the love and understanding I had continued to give him, even though he felt he had made mistakes that should no longer make him worthy of such love. He had felt such remorse for all he had done. He ended this three-page letter telling me that he was proud to have me for a mother and proud that he was my son.

Tears fell to the floor as I read, "I Love you mom. From your son Tony: I hope to see you soon."

How grateful I was that my father had taken those sacks from the apartment. It didn't matter to me that the letter was never sent. To do so meant that Tony would have to make changes and I knew he was not quite ready.

Many things set off tears over the next few months, and even years to come. Each time I would return to the letter. Each time his letter would help me through one more day.

Learning From One Another

My son passed away on a Saturday morning. We held his funeral on the following Tuesday, and because I was the primary financial support for five surviving children, it was necessary for me to return to work on Wednesday. I worked as a full-time, on-call float nurse. I received my assignment each morning in the staffing office of the hospital where I worked. I knew the next few days would be especially difficult, going from one unit to another. Floating was stressful all by itself.

When I entered the staffing office that Wednesday morning, I was told that all the charge nurses for the different units of the hospital had unanimously agreed that I was not to float. They had given me a six-week assignment on the respiratory unit, which was, without contest, my most favorite unit to work. Even kinder is that I was to work no weekends for that space of time, so that I could be with my children, and I was not to be cancelled for those six weeks, even if the hospital census was to drop. I did not have words enough to express my gratitude for this act of compassion, especially since the hospital had taken up a collection, so that I would have enough money to make up for the days of work I had already missed.

Working as an on-call nurse, I was able to work dayshift but working on-call meant that I received no sick time or vacation time. Raising six children on my own also meant that there was never extra money on payday to build up a savings account.

My fellow nurses were sympathetic and caring towards me, especially that first day back. Being nurses, they were all familiar with death. Each one had lost a patient at one time or another and they knew how important it was to comfort those left to mourn. In most settings people just don't know what to say and usually are afraid that they might say the wrong thing. Because of my own son's passing, I learned that being able to talk about death is crucial and is the first step towards being able to heal. I will always remember the events of those first days back and the lessons that were learned from one another.

Gabby was one of the first people to greet me that morning as I walked onto the respiratory unit. She was an outstanding nurse and I had learned so much from her during my times floating there. She was always kind to me. I was a new graduate from nursing school. She taught me how to remove chest tubes, and how to assist with difficult procedures. She taught me how to cope when I would watch one of our patients die from AIDS or be near to a family when their loved one was removed from life support.

But on that day, she taught me that time will ease the grief, but time will never erase the memory. It was at lunch time that she handed me a check. She said that she and her husband had talked it over and that it would mean a lot to them both if I would accept it. I knew that one of the checks that I had received in the card attached to the beautiful spray of flowers from the hospital had her signature on it, so of course I protested.

"No, Gabby, you've already given me so much," I argued.

"But you don't understand," she pleaded. "This means so much to me. You see, Kim, I too lost my son when he was just 17. He died in a terrible car accident just like your son. The only difference is that he was not the driver on that day." She spoke quietly, sadly. "I was."

Gabby was there over those next six weeks, to give me hope, and to help me on the difficult days. We spent time at lunch together, talking and sharing many tears.

She was there for me on the day that I realized I was not as strong as I thought I was. A physician had walked onto our unit and took a seat at the nurse's station where Gabby and I were doing our charting. He was waiting for his wife, who was a nurse on the unit, to be free for her lunch break. He was a surgeon and it was obvious, as he spoke, that his day was not going well.

While speaking to the other doctors dictating at the desk, he announced, "I'm so sick and tired of stitching these young kids back together. Half of them don't care and the boy I worked on this morning probably won't make it!"

It was just too soon to hear those words, I suppose. My thoughts went to the morgue, there looking at my son's face, so that I could identify him; then to his car, as we viewed it for the first time, and to his casket as they lowered its lid for the last time. There I sat, as the tears started to trickle down my cheeks, and within moments, I could not hold them back. I started sobbing right where I sat, embarrassed for what was happening and too numb to speak.

"What is the matter?" the surgeon asked.

Gabby, quick to my rescue and able to feel my pain, put her arms around me. "She lost her son, less than two weeks ago," she explained. "Some of those kids you are stitching back together have families, and sometimes, doctor, those kids make critical mistakes!"

Gabby could have lost her job for speaking to a doctor in such a manner. What happened next surprised us all. The surgeon stood there for a moment looking at me. I was extremely embarrassed during this scene and wanted to be anywhere but there at the desk.

The surgeon walked around to the side where I was sitting. "I am so very sorry," he said. "I did not know."

He was sincere as he reached out his arms to me. I accepted his offer and was scooped up by his caring arms in a consoling embrace. His voice softened as he told me, "I do not know what I would do if I ever lost my own son."

I saw this surgeon from time to time. In my heart, I know there were times when he remembered that day. I have often wondered if he can comprehend what it means to a mother like Gabby or myself that his hands are gifted, and that they may have the skill from day-to-day to determine another child's fate.

Promises

Loving memories are all I have of my father because of how he embraced life while he was here. My nickname was "Sis." My sister's was "Squirt." I remember how he wrapped his right arm firmly around me and squeezed me tight. Dad was a hugger.

He was a prankster, too. The "Sea Scouts" were paid only

25 cents to throw me and my sister into the lake one summer. That was the same summer I learned to water ski. It only took me 46 tries to actually ski around the lake. Dad pretended the boat was malfunctioning, just so he could watch me sink out in the middle.

The next year he dove off a 30-foot-high dive at a different lake, then dared me to do the same. I was much too frightened when I saw the water below and started back down the ladder.

"You're a coward, Sis!" he challenged.

So, I jumped off from the top instead of diving. I nearly took a jump to Heaven that day when I frantically struggled to make it back to the water's surface.

My dad was a generous man, always helping the neighbors. I suppose that growing up during the Depression, on a farm, and having eight siblings made him that way. He moved me and my family more times than I care to remember. He never complained. I was 100 miles from home when I froze the motor of my car. We then had a little chat about why cars have oil lights. He then taught me how to change the oil and the tires.

My dad was a veteran. He begged his father to let him join the Navy at the age of 17. It was during World War II.

"If you can get two uniformed officers to come to my door and tell me why I should let one of my only two sons join, then you can go," were Grandpa's words.

Two days later that happened. I know the war was a hell that no 17-year-old farm boy should have had to experience. My dad always teared up when anybody asked him about those years.

Dad loved my family. He was concerned about who I might marry and worried that the new husband would not love my little son as Grandpa did. Dad hoped I would never walk down that isle. He always wanted to protect Tony. He cried when he spoke at Tony's funeral.

My father married my mother when she was only 16. Though my mother was an exceedingly difficult person, my father remained married to her for 61 years. I asked him why he remained with her after years of quarreling and turmoil.

His words were soft. "Back in my day, when you made a promise, you kept it."

My dad was physically strong. He worked with concrete and marble all his life. His hands were always cracked and sore. He could build a house by himself. He helped other men obtain their carpenters licenses. He never took the test himself because of a learning disability, but he was content knowing he had helped others.

My dad jumped out of a plane on one birthday in his sixties. He embraced life.

Dad did not know the silent killer that would destroy his lungs one day. No one knew that marble dust was like breathing powdered glass. No one wore masks in those early years. It was so hard to see my once powerfully strong father lose his strength and stamina. He eventually had to use oxygen all the time. He was never bitter. He was just sad.

We both grieved as we saw role reversal. My dad remained close to Heavenly Father all his life. He knew his time here upon the earth was soon to end. His main concern was for my mother. He was worried she had burned too many bridges in her life and there would be no one willing to take care of her. I am sure he prayed often about her plight. My mother passed away unexpectedly two weeks before my dad did.

My dad was everything to me. He was always encouraging me and continually positive during my many failures. He always told me to stand back up and try again. When he reached his final years, it was me who was offering encouragement.

"What am I good for?" he questioned.

"You are good for me, Dad," I answered.

My mother's death gave me two weeks to focus on my Father. We were able to ask him about the things he cherished most in life. When alone with him and because I was a nurse, I was able to ask him about his death; he knew it was near.

He was so afraid to die. I could not envision my dad gasping for air. I never wanted to see him panic for his last breath, so I worked closely with hospice to make sure his doctor ordered enough medicines to help him pass gently. I promised him I would be there at his side.

I had just returned to my home after my mother's funeral on a Sunday afternoon in May. My father knew his time was approaching and asked me to come back. It was not an inconvenience jumping right back in my car. I traveled 240 miles, hoping only to arrive in time. I remembered my promise to my dad. I cried all the way back to his home, reflecting on all the things he stood for.

I remembered the things he taught me, and on that day, his last day, I would show him he taught me well. For I, like him, would keep my promise.

A Change of Heart

I have seen great healing during my years as a nurse. Some has been brought about by prayer. Other healing has happened because of medical science. On this most interesting day, the healing was not for my patient, but for his daughter and happened with a most amazing change of heart.

One of my patients passed away only two hours into my shift. I was surprised to see no one was there in his room as he took his final breath. I never had the chance to know anything about him as he was in a coma when I started my shift.

It was my responsibility to call his family to tell them he had died. I always dreaded those calls. Most times you wanted to crawl right through that phone cord and give the person, a long, compassionate hug. I was caught off guard this time with the simple, curt response to my call.

"I won't be coming to the hospital so just send his body to the mortuary."

I thought of past times and past patients and how sad I always felt when they died alone. I did not judge but instead went about the task of preparing his body. With that completed, I did as his daughter asked, and called the mortuary.

Hours went by but the people from the mortuary did not come. Then a lady ran quickly to the nurses' station and asked for "Kim."

"Is it too late?" she said, struggling to catch her breath. "Has the mortuary taken my father away?"

She was so relieved when I explained to her that they were late but coming soon. "Oh, may I please see him?" Her affect had indeed changed.

She paused as we neared his room and shared a most amazing story. "My father was a mean man," she stated. "He was horrible to mother and to all of my siblings. He never had a kind word for anyone. He has no friends because he is a friend to no one. He drank away his paycheck and our lives were difficult.

"The hospital called me at two this morning to tell me my father had slipped into a coma," she said in a whispered voice. "I was just returning to bed when the phone rang again at 2:15, only 15 minutes later. It was my father. His voice was clear, and his words were concise. He said he loved me. He said he was sorry. Sorry for everything.

"My father lived alone in a tiny trailer. He told me where he had hidden a key to its door. His insurance policies and safe were exactly where he said they would be. I didn't believe him until I went to his home this morning.

"This is all so amazing," she continued. "You would have had to know my father. More amazing is that at 2:30 I called the hospital. They said he was still unresponsive, and there had been no change.

"Oh, but there had been. I guess my siblings and I will be the only ones to believe that our father—mean as he was—had indeed been overcome by a most wonderful change, a most welcomed change of heart."

The Challenge of Saying Goodbye

I remember my toughest nursing challenge. It happened in the Mother-Baby unit not so long ago. Mr. and Mrs. Garcia requested that a nurse dress their tiny twins, Julie and Jessica. Each little girl had lived less than an hour and their parents had chosen beautiful miniature dresses for the cremation.

As I entered their room, it became obvious that Mr. Garcia was grieving. His cheeks were still moist from tears.

"He wants you to handle the babies very carefully," the interpreter said.

Realizing that these were his last moments with his daughters, my eyes also began to tear up.

"Mr. Garcia," I said, "not long ago, my own son died. He was only 17. I chose his favorite cream and blue sweater. I held him in my arms and gently dressed his broken body. Oh, Mr. Garcia, I will touch your babies as tenderly as my own."

He kissed each little daughter and left the room with a quiet "Thank you." A few minutes later, there was a knock on the door. Mrs. Garcia's ride had arrived. As I started to take the babies away, I turned back to see tears flooding her eyes.

"Mrs. Garcia," I said, "You will always be their Mother. Please take all of the time you need to tell your little ones just how much they will be missed."

As I left her room, I knew my own son's tragic death had taught me to show others how to whisper a final goodbye.

4 THE TREE BEARS FRUIT (WHEN TOUCHED BY THE SPIRIT)

I have likened my life unto that of a tree. The first seedlings found their beginnings in rich heritage and amazing miracles in my early life. These seedlings took root with Angels round about me, protecting me and allowing me to find an anchor in hope and faith. I began to see glimpses of what God had always intended me to become. I was able to stand strong even through the storms of death and loss. More was to come.

From the tiniest and most timid little thing, I began to blossom. I began to see myself through God's eyes. I would never have imagined that my growth would have taken me from a frightened young mother of six to a lady who was able to take charge and see the needs of others. I would liken that growth to a beautiful blossoming fruit tree: there to give succor, there to give shade, and there to give protection from gusty winds and the storms of life.

I have been so humbled to know that my kind Heavenly Father has trusted me to be inspired so that I may know through the power of the Holy Ghost, when one of His children is in need of my help. I know that if I remain close to Him, He will guide me to those who need protection. My greatest joy would be to give you hope, as my Father has done for me, with His arms wrapped eternally around you.

Heavenly Insurance Premiums

Each year as December ends, making way for a New Year and a new beginning, I am always reminded of what a wonderful blessing it is to pay tithing. I feel a quiet closeness to my Father in Heaven when I realize that such a private commitment to righteousness has brought me closer to Him in so many ways.

Many years ago, when I was studying to become a nurse, Patriarch Hall and his dear wife appointed themselves to be my "home teachers," special people in my congregation who serve others. I was struggling with the stress of knowing that my future and my family's future was solely in my hands. Patriarch Hall saw things differently however, and with hands placed upon my head, gave me a powerful blessing that I would never forget. He promised me that I would be successful in my endeavors if I would always pay my tithing and put my nursing studies aside on Sunday.

My tithing was a mere $50. However, my blessings could never be measured for there were so many. As I put my Father in Heaven first, ahead of all worldly considerations, he blessed us to the point that all our needs were answered often and in exact ways.

One time the lady down the street came to our door with an arm full of jeans. She never knew that I had been on my knees the night before, asking Father how I was to replace my little sons' ratty ones. Our little blue beater of a car did not cough out its last sputter until two weeks before graduation. Oh, it died many, many times, but five-year-old Katie, always insisted we fold arms and pray, and the "Blue bomb" would start right up again. "Grandma Granger," as we lovingly called her, would always call us when there were extra donuts at the William Temple House, pears left to pick in the orchards, or shoes that were to be donated by the Lions Club.

Shortly after my graduation, the Lord once again showed our little family that His promises are sure. It was in the spring of 1987. We had some unexpected expenses come our way. To this day, I cannot remember what they were, but I never forgot what happened. When it came time to pay the bills, my paycheck simply was not enough. We were short by $150 and did not have enough money to buy food. I was worried. My tithing was the same amount. Over and over in my mind, I thought about the options. Realizing there wasn't one, I made out all the bills and I paid my tithing. Then I prayed. And then I prayed some more. I had to put my complete trust in Heavenly Father. Even as I placed those paid bills into the mailbox, I simply did not know how we would find a way to pay for food.

The next morning, I called the hospital where I worked to see if our paychecks were ready to be picked up.

The payroll secretary was so excited! "Kim, did you hear your name called on the radio station this morning?"

She told me how they had drawn my name on KWJJ's grocery grab. You see, I had been sending in my grocery receipts every two weeks for almost two years. If your grocery receipt was drawn and you called the radio station back within an hour, you received double the amount of your receipt. If you did not hear your name called, the radio station sent you the amount on the grocery receipt. What was the amount on my grocery receipt? One hundred and fifty dollars and thirty cents!

To this day, tithing is always paid first, no matter what my bills are. I feel that tithing is my Heavenly Insurance Policy. Even when the bills don't add up correctly on my ledger, I promise you, they always do on His.

The Lord Chose My Assignment

It was a crisp Portland spring Sunday morning many, many years ago. I carefully put on the final touches to my makeup. My mind drifted as I thought how wonderful it would be to sleep in like other mothers...and...just for today, be a stay at home mom. I would take the time to make pancakes and then be off to church with my children.

My daydream was interrupted by the ringing of the phone. The voice on the line was all too familiar. "Sorry Kim, we need to cancel you this morning."

A flood of emotions swept over me as I quietly placed the phone in its holder. There was joy in knowing that I could now sleep in. It was my third shift to be cancelled in one week and I was not one of those "other" moms. I was a single parent, with five adolescent children. I was the breadwinner, the anchor, and the provider for my family.

I felt panic and anxiety as I lowered to my knees on the drafty bedroom floor. I paused for a moment to calm my soul and quietly reflect on all my many blessings. I thought of the many doors that had been unlocked for me. I remembered the three difficult years of nursing school, struggling with being newly divorced and alone with six children. He had been my Savior in the truest sense during the recent death of my oldest son. He was always nearby. I felt His spirit close and His arms wrapped around me often. He knew each struggle and had answered every prayer, sometimes in such profound ways that I could never call them coincidences. He helped me to remain humble.

"Please, Heavenly Father. I need your help," I prayed. I lovingly reminded Him that my children could not grow up if I could not feed them. (I always knew the Lord enjoyed my sense of humor). And then at that moment a powerful feeling encompassed my being and I still remember my words to this day: "I'll take any assignment you want me to. I will go anywhere. I promise."

It was six-thirty when the phone rang once again. The registry took a late sick call from one of the community hospitals, a hospital I had never worked at before. It was out in the country. They needed a nurse on the Post-Surgical floor.

"Would you be willing to go, Kim?"

I thought of my promise as I hung up the phone. I grabbed my stethoscope. Shaking it gently above my head, I glanced upward. "I hope you realize who you are sending."

I was always nervous the first time I accepted an assignment at a hospital. My stomach was twisted into knots. You would have thought I was the one who needed a nurse.

Walking onto the third floor, the charge nurse quickly greeted me with the most beautiful smile and a wonderfully reassuring voice. "What can we do to make this assignment work for our unit and for you today?"

After a quick tour of the unit, I was on my own. She had carefully chosen my assignment. Mrs. Ford was going home that day. Mr. Jackson was one day post-op and Mr. Carlsen was recovering from his surgery just the evening before.

Mrs. Ford was anxious to get home, so I completed her discharge teaching first. I requested she put her light on when her ride arrived to take her home.

Next, I knocked on Mr. Carlsen's door. There was no answer. Knocking again, I poked my head just inside. He sat there in bed, with his brow tensely creased.

"Mr. Carlsen, my name is Kim. I will be your nurse today."

He looked miserable. When I asked if he needed something for pain, he cut me short. His words were deliberate. "Demerol won't fix my pain! Nothing will! You wouldn't understand anyway."

My five short years of nursing had taught me a lot about pain relief. The best hypodermic was ofttimes a listening ear.

Reflective listening could unlock doors to a patient's suffering that seemed like an insurmountable barricade against you. I confessed that I might not totally understand his situation, but I assured him I was there with time to listen.

His countenance calmed. His brow softened. The door gently opened and soon this sweet man poured out rapids of emotion. The hurt and pain inside of him were like a river tumbling over the edge, like falls flowing down with anger. He could not fight its force any longer. He shared the pain of his impending divorce and the recent loss of his hopes and dreams. How hurt he was from this ended marriage. Any surgical pain seemed small in comparison.

We talked. We listened. We shared. I too had walked in similar shoes. I remember the emptiness and sorrow I felt as I started life over again, numb from broken promises and fearful of what lie ahead.

Putting the nurse-patient relationship aside for the moment, I confided "If it had not been for my church and all the kind, sweet singles there, I don't know if I would have made it through my divorce." I felt a bit embarrassed, as we were talking friend to friend.

He lifted his eyes to meet mine, and with barriers down, he asked, "What church do you belong to?"

No sooner had the name of the church left my mouth that he picked up a book that was resting on his bedside stand. He stated that two young men had given him the book and would be returning to see him "after he felt up to it."

I was then, and even now, a quiet and shy individual, yet I took the book right out of his hand. With a strength and power of conviction that could not have been mine alone, I joyfully exclaimed, "Oh My Goodness! Have you read this book?" My finger raced for a scripture that I knew by memory and recited the promise to him as he read along with me.

Once again, he lifted his eyes to meet mine.

"Peter, if you read this book and pray about it, I promise you, you will never feel empty again."

Time was moving on and I had one more patient to see.

Leaving Peter's room, I felt peaceful. I felt no concern about sharing my testimony. The power that had engulfed me was difficult to explain in words. I felt certain that what had just happened was meant to be.

Mr. Jackson was my third patient. He had recently broken his leg. His wife was near his side as I entered the room. I asked them how he had sustained such an injury.

Mrs. Jackson's humor made the best of the situation. "We have been gone overseas for months now, on a mission for our church. We never had one mishap. But President Jackson had to make a grand entrance for his homecoming. He fell down the ramp as we got off the plane!"

What a coincidence that this couple were members of my church. I must tell you that the synchronizing of events did not end there. I told Brother Jackson about my other patient and his visit from the missionaries. With a grand smile sweeping over his face, he reached for the Sunday Oregonian, that day's newspaper. He handed me a full-page selection entitled *Meet the Mormons*.

"Please," Brother Jackson said, "give this to your patient."

Things just kept getting better! Mr. Carlsen's door was open, and I knocked gently. Stepping into the room, I apologized as soon as I saw he was on the phone and turned around to leave.

"Just a minute, Kim," he said. "I have the missionaries on the phone. They say there is full page write up about your church in the newspaper today."

Now the smile was on my face. With two hands extending the article, I replied, "This one?"

Mr. Carlsen put down the phone for a moment. "This has got to be a conspiracy!" he joked.

Mrs. Ford went home early that day. Brother Jackson was to go home the next. As time neared for me to end my shift, I stopped by one last time to say good-bye to Peter. The shower could be heard running in the bathroom. I gently pulled a piece of paper down from the towel dispenser near the sink. I wrote a little note on it and taped it to his bedside stand. It read,

"Please! Read the book."

Two months later, on a beautiful Sunday evening, I felt prompted—so prompted—to go to the Singles Fireside at my church some 40 minutes away. I rarely went because I wanted to spend my precious time with my children. After the meeting, I was anxious to return to them and decided to decline any refreshments.

I was almost out the door when I heard my name called. There in the foyer, a man near my age quickly came closer to me.

"It's you!" he exclaimed. "You are the one. You are the nurse!"

Seeing that I was taken back, he slowed down. With a worried voice he said, "You don't remember me, do you?"

Then eye-to-eye and soul-to-soul, with a warm smile that replaced all sadness, he explained with such sincerity, "I swear, Kim. I thought you must have been crazy to be as bold as you were, so I simply had to read that book. I am so glad to see you here tonight. I am getting baptized. Oh Kim, can you come?"

I was totally overcome with tears. Not until that **very** moment, did I realize that on that cold, crisp spring Sunday morning, it was **Heavenly Father** who had chosen my assignment.

A Heavenly Intervention

Several years ago, I came to know that people can be used as a conduit to give messages that we need to hear from heaven.

One day I worked a shift on the surgical unit. I walked into a semi-private room to introduce myself to two of my assigned patients. After meeting the lady next to the window and quickly surmising that she was confused, I did an about face to meet the patient next to the door. Before I could complete my introduction, I was interrupted with "DO YOU BELIEVE IN JESUS CHRIST!" blurted out by the lady next to the window. "Of course, I do," was my answer. And then again, "DO YOU GO TO CHURCH?" "Yes," I softly stated, trying to calm her down. "I belong and go to The Church of Jesus Christ of Latter-Day Saints." There was silence as she settled down and began eating her breakfast once more, and thankfully remained quiet.

I was then able to greet my other patient. We both looked at each other with raised eyebrows, wondering what might be the next words to come out of our confused lady's mouth.

"So, you are a member of the church?" she inquired.

I cheerfully asked her if she was also. Indeed, she was. She was a member of a different congregation (or "ward," as we call them).

I told her how my husband and I enjoyed having the missionaries (or "elders," as we call them) live in the basement of our home and the sweet spirit they brought with them. She told me how she used to have the elders over for dinner.

She turned her eyes away from mine as she confessed quietly, "I haven't been to church for a while now and haven't had them to dinner for a long time. You know I am having surgery tomorrow?"

She continued, "I will go to intensive care after the operation because of all of my health problems. I don't know how my husband will manage if something happens to me."

She was overwhelmed with worry. She had reason to be. She was to have a complicated, long, and dangerous surgery.

"Are you nervous?" I asked. She did not want to let me know just how afraid she was. She did not have to. I already knew. "Do you want a blessing?"

"Oh, I'm not worthy," she countered.

"Are you sick? I know you are frightened." I continued, "Then, you are certainly worthy."

I was her nurse, and the elders rented our basement. Now that was an awesome combination. We made sure her roommate was taken on a walk so her room would be quiet as the elders arrived.

She was blessed with comfort. She was blessed with strength and told that strength would be necessary in the months to follow. She was promised patience and a thankful heart. Her daughter was present for the blessing and heard as they promised her mom that if she "had faith enough, she would eventually have her health restored." They embraced one another with tears streaming down their faces.

Those words would come to pass. Her first surgery was extensive and diagnosed more health issues that needed future surgical intervention. I recognized the daughter immediately when she frantically searched the hospital units looking for me. Her mother was soon to have the second surgery.

"Could you...well, Kim...would you mind?"

Soon the elders were by the family's side once more and each time when requested. I was not at all surprised to hear that the elders were once again seated at their dinner table and lovingly helping them secure rides to church.

As for her roommate, well she was cheerful and oriented from that morning on. Sometimes, I suppose, the Holy Ghost needs to make a grand entrance when **"A Heavenly Intervention"** is required.

Some things are simply not coincidences, but happen because Heavenly Father uses us as an instrument in his hands...

In the Right Place at the Right Time

Usually as a nurse, I use the words person, place and time, as a way of describing a person's level of orientation. Does my patient know who he is, where he is, and does he know what time it is? On this day, those words had a much different meaning, and I came to know that I was the right person, in the right place at just the right time.

My day at the hospital started out like most others had in the last 14 years, way too early, far from home, and again greeted by a chorus of wailing newborns. I was just getting to know my patients for that day. I had been talking at length with a new young mother. To tell you the truth, I can't remember now how most of the conversation went, but I do remember telling her that all new parents will make their share of mistakes raising their children, especially in the beginning. I told her how even God knew we would, and that He still made the decision to send His sweet little spirits on loan out to us because He has unlimited hope for their futures.

When I walked out of my patient's room, I was greeted by a young lady in her late teens or early twenties who was assigned to be our nurse's aide that day. She followed me as I went up to the front desk.

"You are Mormon, aren't you?" she inquired.

I was puzzled that she was asking because I had never met her before. She went on to tell me that she had heard some of my conversation as she walked past my patient's room. I told her that I was, and since I was curious, I asked her if she was too. She told me that she was a member of my church but had not gone for quite some time. She also shared with me that she felt her dad was disappointed with her decision not to attend. She confided in me that she rarely talked to him anymore because she did not want to bring him any more disappointment. It was easy to see how much love and respect she had for her father. I could tell she was hurting. I asked her to take her lunchbreak with me so we could talk some more. She had no way of knowing that I—not long ago—had been hurting too.

Four hours passed between then and noon. Four hours

gave me plenty of time to think about my own dad. I had prayed for two long years that Heavenly Father would intervene in the shattered relationship between my father and me. I knew firsthand that not all things go smoothly in life, especially relationships. It had been just two months earlier that Dad had been in a head-on collision with a young teenage boy who crossed the center line. I did not know that the mending would start in a hospital room in a trauma center. I welcomed the chance, however, to be at his side once more. I knew that not everyone is given a second chance like we were.

I met with Rachel in the breakroom and, to our thankful surprise, we were able to share our lunch undisturbed. Rachel was most certainly in need of a spiritual friend. She did not know how to break the ice with her dad. She was not sure that he would understand her confusion about how to choose what direction to take in her life. She had always seen her father as a leader within her church community and in her home. *Perhaps he was stern and unforgiving*, I wondered. I knew though that I had no right to judge or to pry. I asked her if she had ever received her Patriarchal Blessing. She told me that she never had because she never felt close enough to Heavenly Father to have one. A Patriarchal Blessing is given to a person usually just once in their lifetime.

After fasting and prayer, a Latter-Day Saint member meets with the Patriarch in their geographical location for a beautiful blessing. With hands placed upon their head, and through Heavenly Father's inspiration, the Patriarch pronounces a blessing for the life of that person. It may have warnings and admonitions to give direction. It also helps the person to understand how Heavenly Father sees them, their talents and possible goals. It is a blessing of promise and of hope. I had mine when I was 19. I cherish its counsel and advice to this day.

As I talked with Rachel, I could see that she was struggling to make right decisions but had not felt successful. She told me of some recent errors in judgment. I told her of mine—almost 50 years old, still making mistakes, still learning from them. I told her how wonderful it was to have two fathers in this lifetime to care about the things we do. I told her how empty I felt without my earthly father for those struggling years. I told her how it was such a wonderful alliance: Heavenly Father working with our earthly parents to help us to return to Him someday.

I asked Rachel if she might consider calling her father. I told her it wouldn't be such a bad idea if she placed a local call to her earthly father and then placed that long distance call to Heavenly Father. I told her it wouldn't cost anything, and she should not keep them waiting any longer.

Rachel sought me out at about two-thirty that afternoon. She was certainly excited. She had called her father at work. He was surprised. He was happy. He made a date to take her to lunch the following afternoon. Rachel radiated joy. As we shared hugs, I felt her excitement. I remembered how it felt to have my own father back once more.

Before she turned to go back to work, she said, "I'll be placing the other phone call tonight. I want to ask Him about blessings."

I thought of Rachel later that night as I knelt on my own knees. I thanked our Heavenly Father for the wonderful blessing of being the right person, in the right place, at exactly the right time.

My Saving Grace

I lived in Battleground, Washington for six years. The decision to move there in 1992 provided my five teenagers with great schools for their education. It was wonderful to live in the country and it would prove to be the town where one son and one daughter would find their mate. The only disadvantage was the commute across the river to my job in Oregon every day.

As my youngest neared graduation, I decided to move closer to Oregon. When my search began, I started looking for a home with a large yard and one with neighbors not so far away. I was also looking for a home with a finished basement that could be shared with family members if they needed help from "mom."

I looked at many homes, and usually found that what I was searching for wasn't available at rent I could afford. Early in my search, I found an older home but I kept putting it out of my mind because I really wanted something newer. A couple months went by and as I continued to look, my thoughts kept coming back to that quaint little house. One day with its key in hand, it welcomed me in again. This time I envisioned its walls with my pictures, its windows with my curtains, and I felt with warm anticipation that this was to be *home*.

My youngest son Bjarne was able to get a job at Oregon Health Sciences University during that summer. He decided to make the move with me since we now worked the same shift at the same hospital. We would both save money commuting together. I never had time to feel lonely in the beginning. Doing errands by day and working in the evening kept me busy. All too soon my shift changed back to days. Bjarne was at work when I came home. I was asleep when he got home. It was difficult.

Having four of my five teenagers move out on their own in a space of only five years made my heart ache. I missed my children. I missed being needed by them. I soon came to realize that they had been my life, my reason for working, and my reason for laughter. They had given my life purpose. I was so shy. I always had been. I was not the type of person to ask another over to my house or go on a lunch date. My best friends were my children. I had not needed closer friends because my own children kept me so busy.

I became so lonely that at times I was tearful. I needed a friend. I wanted one desperately. I knew Heavenly Father was aware that I was grieving. Although my nest was not quite empty, I knew it would be soon. It was only time before my Bjarne would be spreading his wings as his brothers and sisters had done. One day I petitioned Father in Heaven. I dropped to my knees and told him my plight. "Please send someone my way. I am so lonely and could use a friend."

The next day was to be like any other—or so I thought. I pulled my car into the "park and ride" just after six a.m., like all work mornings. I had been running late. The bus left quickly as I took my seat. I had a book for that morning's ride, but instead closed my tired eyes for a few more winks on the 25-minute commute. A voice was heard in and out of my efforts to rest. I had heard it before, so I opened my eyes. I searched for the voice's owner and soon located her.

She was about my age. She had a pan of homemade rolls in her hand. She looked like a nurse, dressed in scrubs, the same as me. But her voice—I could not put a face with it. I just knew her voice was familiar to me. I sat there and listened as she talked. Where had I met her before? I knew I had. I closed my eyes and quietly asked God to help me remember. Suddenly it came to me. *Was it really her?* I was too shy to ask, but I wanted to know. She was sitting right across from me.

I didn't want to be rude but when her conversation was over, I quickly asked, "Is your name Grace?"

"Some call me Virginia, but I also go by Grace," she replied.

"Grace, it's Kim," I exclaimed. "Do you remember me, from Portland, back in the seventies? You're a member of my church."

Before long we were striking up quite the conversation. We had been friends when our children were just babies. She and her husband Bill had relocated, and we lost touch with one another. We each had added several more children to our little families. Neither one of us were nurses back then. There we were working at adjoining hospitals, riding the same bus. We were in the same congregation once again in our church.

Grace again became one of my dearest friends as our lives

were reunited. She was the one person I could share my deepest thoughts with. Grace had many friends already, to be sure, and I don't know if to this day she realizes how many times she lifted me up when I was down. Today we live almost 300 miles apart, for I remarried and relocated.

That little home became my haven and a haven for many. It took in my children, my grandchildren and even my children's closest friends. Some people might say it was just a coincidence that Grace's home was less than four blocks away. I do not think so, for my Heavenly Father knows me and that little house beckoning me was God's way of showing me He was there. He always will be there.

Songs of the Heart

Twenty years of nursing has brought many patients into my life. Some were there for only a fleeting moment, while others were in my company for a time longer, all depending on the seriousness of their illness. There have also been those who have touched my life, not by the length of their hospital stay but by the bonds that united our hearts. This was the case with Mr. Randall.

He was introduced to me by his family when I entered his hospital room. He was confused and disoriented. According to the nursing staff, "pleasantly confused" was a better description, as he had occupied himself most of the previous night by singing songs. His family was caring and supportive. They expounded on how difficult it was to see their father in this state, relating that he was an exceptionally bright man. He had many talents, I was told, but most praise-worthy was that of being a choir director. The entire family commented on "how much Dad loves to sing."

Later that day, I was able to slip into his room during a quiet period on our unit, which was indeed a rare occurrence! Mr. Randall was humming a beautiful love song entitled "Let Me Call You Sweetheart." I joined his humming with the actual words to the song. Soon his humming gave way to words, and our voices blended in perfect harmony.

As the last note was sung, he quickly remarked, "I'll bet you don't know this one."

For more than half an hour we harmonized to the old Mitch Miller tunes, love songs of the thirties and forties, and ballads of his time. He was clear and alert, never missing a note.

I hated the fact that I had to return to my work as I had five other patients that day. I was, however, grateful that we were able to share together the great love we both had for music on that Saturday afternoon. Nurses back at the nurses' station joked with me about my "new type of therapy," but I didn't mind. I thought how wonderful it had been to step into his world and put mine behind for those few precious moments. Mr. Randall was sleeping when I left for home early that evening. I did not wake him to say good-bye.

Four months later I would again introduce myself to Mr. Randall. When I walked into my patient's room, the family standing around the bed looked familiar to me.

They recognized me immediately. "It's good to see you again, Kim. Dad talked for weeks about the nurse who sang with him last November."

My eyes left the family as I excitedly turned to greet Mr. Randall. This time there was no smile. There were no words, not one sound. There against the white sheets lay a whisper of the man I once sang with. Mr. Randall had suffered a massive stroke. He could not move. He could not speak. Occasionally his eyes would open and gaze upon loved ones about the room. My heart broke for Mr. Randall, for his family and for myself.

Amy was my aide that day. I loved working with Amy. She spoke to her patients with care even if there was a doubt that they could understand her. I always admired her for that. We had to roll Mr. Randall from side to side every two hours to prevent the hard bed from creating pressure sores on his tender skin. The family members had stepped out for a break for a while and as the two of us rolled Mr. Randall from his side to his back, I could stand it no longer.

"It's worth a try," I said to myself. I then asked Amy if she sang.

"Well, that depends," she said. She pulled a chair up to one side of the bed and I to the other. Amy took Mr. Randall's hand.

"I want to try one song first and then we'll do one together."

I sang slowly and tenderly, "Let me call you sweetheart..." word by word until I could barely manage it any longer, as Amy's cheeks soon became streaked with tears. We had Mr. Randall's full attention and his eyes watched both of us.

I started the next song. "You are my sunshine..." Amy joined in. "...my only sunshine." and together we sang, "You make me happy when skies are grey." Then to our amazement we watched as his lips mouthed the words. Oh, so slowly and carefully, we sang so he could follow. "You'll never know dear, how much I love you."

He mouthed one word, then two but then on the chorus, each word was mouthed "You" "Are" "My" "Sunshine..." We sang all three verses. Mr. Randall caught a word here and there, but on each chorus, never missed one note..."Please don't take my sunshine away!" Tears tumbled off all cheeks, for a song is only a song, of course, unless...it was sung from our hearts.

Go Today

To Know He Is There

I love Multnomah Falls. Tucked into the cliffs off the Columbia Gorge Highway, it is easy to miss if you are solely content on driving and not on sight-seeing. Its water tumbles some 640 feet to create a beautiful pond that is easily seen from a magnificent bridge near the end of its journey.

I had hiked Multnomah Falls many times, sometimes with a date, sometimes with my children. One thing was for certain. It took a long time to climb to the top of the falls. It was steep and easily left you panting for air for your next breath. It took even longer for the elderly or those physically unfit. I usually fell into the latter category, but not on this warm summer day, for I had shed some 60 pounds.

From the beginning of summer that year, I had thought what a challenge it would be to make it to the top without stopping a single time. Knowing that, I easily pushed it out of my mind each time. This day was no different but, for some reason, I kept being prompted repeatedly to jump into my convertible and go.

Just getting there was fun. With the car's top down, the warm air felt great as it hit my face. With water in hand, I thought to myself, "This will be an amazing day." And it was. Mind you, there were times I was tempted to stop for a while, but I didn't, and that felt even better.

The trail winding one direction and then another, was crowded with people nearing the top of the Falls. I knew there were trails even further up with streams of cool water tumbling over rocks and logs. Not many people ventured further in that direction. Perhaps they did not know they could or maybe they were content enough having reached the top, or what they thought was the top.

As I traveled a bit further along the trail, I heard what seemed to be the laughter of several children, having fun. It did not take long however to realize that it was not laughter I was hearing, but the cries of many children for help. My feet ran faster than I knew they could. Soon I saw the panic. Children were running helplessly and crying frantically as a large swarm of hornets, protecting their nest, made the children their prey.

To Know He Is There

A day camp's outdoor fun soon turned into a nightmare.

One boy about age eight or nine had multiple welts on his arms and face. All the children were stung, but this little boy was ashen in color and I knew he was in trouble. No one had a cell phone to call 911. I closed my eyes and my heart pled to Heavenly Father, "Lord, help us, please."

The camp director hesitated for a moment when I told her she needed to go back to the base of the falls. I knew there would be access to 911 and a park ranger there. I had seen rangers carry someone off the trail on a stretcher on a previous hike. She did not know me. These little ones were her responsibility, after all. She changed her mind quickly when I told her I was a nurse and this little boy needed an epinephrine pen and an ambulance right away or he could die.

An older child who was part of the camp helped me to carry this little boy further up the trail a few feet away from the nest. We told the other children to get into the cool water to treat their stings. We carefully looked at them individually. They became calmer, as they made splashing in the water a game. How worried we were about the little guy who was stung so badly. He was so swollen and becoming listless. Even though it was just a few minutes, it seemed like an eternity before several park rangers arrived. They were quick to see our dilemma, and even quicker to act. We hastened the children out of the water. Stretchers and shoulders carried all those who needed it. An ambulance could be heard at a distance as we neared the scenic bridge.

I have seen amazing things at Multnomah Falls. Once there was a beautiful wedding and vows were exchanged on the splendid bridge, with all of us hoping they would not drop the rings. On another occasion, my friend and I started our date too late one afternoon and were relieved as park rangers, with flashlights, lit our path so we no longer had to hold tight to the cliffs in the dark. Once my own ten-year-old son clung to a bush waiting to scare me as I joined my kids who were further up the trail. He did not care that he could have fallen 100s of feet downward. He achieved his purpose, I must say.

What was coincidental to me is that the day camp was in the town where I lived, Battleground Washington. And why, after contemplating the hike on so many occasions, did I relent to taking the hike on that day?

I will always choose to believe that it was not by chance, but this coincidence, as I once read on a sign at the beach, was God's way of letting me know "He was there."

I Just Thought I Would Call

Working as a nurse, I have had the opportunity to witness many of God's miracles. I have seen the joy that new parents share as they hold their new son or daughter for the first time. Tears fill my eyes each time a spirit enters this world or departs from it. With each such occurrence, I am reminded that the affairs of this life are carefully orchestrated by a gentle and loving God. Every time I witness a baby taking its first breath, I am amazed at the human body, and the process that must take place for that to occur. When I am with a patient who takes that final breath, departing from this life to the next, I feel joy and sorrow all at the same time. More than anything, I feel an awesome reverence. I am sure that our Heavenly Father intervenes when necessary to make certain that we leave this world or enter it when it is our time to do so. I was reminded of this in quite a remarkable way not many years ago.

I was working on the Mother-Baby and Women's Health floor of a renowned hospital in the Portland Metropolitan area. It was just after lunch and I was soon to receive a patient who was the mother of one of our noted gynecologists. I had worked with Dr. Brady in several positions, both as a staff nurse and as a clinic nurse. I admired his gentle nature and the genuine concern he showed for all his patients. Never had I heard him raise his voice. Never was I to witness him speaking negatively of his fellow associates. It was not his nature. I considered it a privilege to be the nurse chosen to take care of Dr. Brady's mother.

When I heard that Mrs. Brady had been a practicing nurse herself for many years, I must admit, I felt a bit nervous. Most nurses do when they take care of those who have R.N. next to their name. I think it is because we worry that any errors that we might make with a fellow peer will not go unnoticed.

I was surprised how well Mrs. Brady transferred from the stretcher to her hospital bed when the orderly brought her from the recovery unit to ours. She was cheerful and alert. She denied having any pain, so I did not connect her to the morphine pump that she would use for pain control. It seemed unusual to me at the time that she was not hurting, as the recovery nurse who gave me the report stated that it had taken a lot of narcotics to make her comfortable right after surgery. I helped her get comfortably situated in her bed and then took her vital signs—temperature, pulse and such. Everything was normal. I then went out to the nurses' station to do a charting note about her arrival. Her next set of vital signs were to be taken 15 minutes later.

Five or ten minutes had passed by when her son Dr. Brady called our unit to check in on "mom." I told him how easily she had transferred from stretcher to bed and that she denied having any pain at all. He wanted to speak to her only if she was awake. I put the phone on hold and went to her room which was just a few steps away. When I entered the room, she appeared to be sleeping. Normally, I would have returned to the desk, but an uneasy feeling came over me and I stepped next to the side of her bed to look closely at her.

For nearly ten seconds, I did not see her chest rise or fall. I called her name. She did not respond. I shook her and still no response. I ran just outside the room. One of residents was just about to walk off our unit and I told him I was calling a code blue. Then I told him the name of my patient. All feet went flying as we raced for the code cart and made an overhead page for the code team. I then remembered that Dr. Brady was still on hold. I told him his mother was not responsive when I had entered her room and that we had already called a code blue.

My heart sank, as I knew he was some 35 minutes away, rounding at a different hospital. I thought how I would feel not knowing the fate of my loved one as I rushed in traffic to be by their side.

All hands worked diligently giving Mrs. Brady narcotic antagonists. It took several minutes before she began to respond. It was several more minutes before she was stable.

The concerned look that encompassed Dr. Brady's face as he entered our unit was one I will not ever forget. The tense, drawn lines of his face eased as we told him his mother was responding. He quickly entered her room and drew a chair up near the side of her bed. He did not leave her side for hours. Each time I checked in on them, their hands were clasped lovingly together. Dr. Brady reassured his mother that everything was going to be just fine each time she opened her eyes.

It was almost evening when Dr. Brady left his mother's room to call home and let his wife and children know what happened. When his call was finished, we stood there for a moment, thinking about what had happened.

"What made you call here at the time you did?" I asked.

"I finished my paperwork sooner than I expected," he said.

We both knew that finishing paperwork early for him was a miracle all by itself, for his desk always had a tower of it waiting for him at the end of clinic. His patients came first; the charting came second. We both knew that his timely call had saved his mother's life. She did not have another five minutes for me to enter her room to check her vital signs. She would have been gone. We both knew that someone that afternoon was watching over her.

I came to know that Mrs. Brady was loved beyond comprehension. I was there to witness just how much. She had a wonderful son to comfort her here in this life and a loving Father to send angels for her protection from beyond the veil that day.

Mrs. Brady stayed with us for three more days before returning home. She was quite the character and quite the nurse. Just before departing out the door of our unit, she tried to make us all feel at ease about her hospitalization.

"My stay was great," she said. With eyebrows raised, she added, "but there is just one question I've been meaning to ask...why did you want to kill me? I mean, really."

We heard her chuckle as the doors closed behind her wheelchair...and we all sighed with sadness at her departure. But I need to add, we also sighed: a sigh of great relief!

The Layoff

On July 1, 1995, it was official, and the finality of our unit's cutbacks was put into place. Six nurses from the Mother-Baby Unit raised our hospital's layoff list to nearly 80. It seems so incredible as I look back on it now, that a layoff took place when only a relatively short time later, there was a nationwide nursing shortage. What seems even more incredible to me was the lesson I learned about trust.

I had two sons in high school, two daughters who were not yet on their own and a little seven-month-old grandson who all depended on me for a roof over their heads and food on the table. There was no savings account to fall back on, no rich uncle and no inheritance coming my way that I knew. I had been given my pink slip—all based on seniority—two weeks prior. There wasn't a day of those 14 that passed by that I did not find myself on my knees asking Heavenly Father what I should do. Each prayer ended with the overwhelming feeling that I should not look for work elsewhere.

Each time I called the hospital hotlines in the area, I felt as though I was being reprimanded and with one such call, I was told so clearly "Put down the phone!" Every time I looked through the want ads, I felt that it was the wrong thing to do. The human part of me thought maybe all these moments were just a form of denial and that the next morning would bring back my job but...that did not happen.

Not only was my job eliminated, but so were my benefits, vacation time, sick pay, and medical coverage. There was no language in the hospital contract that addressed how the laid-off nurses were to be called in for shifts when our unit needed help. Even with all this bad news, a burden upon my shoulders, the words kept coming to my mind, "be still and know I am here." I was soon to find out, God is not absent when it comes to those small life-saving coincidences that build faith and create peace.

The next day I received a phone call saying that they were short staffed at work and the same call came again the next night. They had called the other five nurses and each time they were unable to fill the shift. It was easy to see that several of the laid off nurses were wanting to only work their preferred shift and there was not language in the contract to assign the shifts equally. I asked that our manager meet with all six of us and soon a plan was put into place where we rotated who was called to work, shift by shift, so each of us had to take a turn with an evening shift or night shift as well as days.

Heavenly Father showed me just how sure His promptings truly are. I was working an evening shift about a week after I had been laid off. Catherine worked as a resource nurse on evening shift. I rarely saw her coming onto work when I was leaving after my day shift, and I told her how lucky she was to be working so infrequently. As we continued to talk with one another, I learned that she also worked at the Women's Health Clinic located within the hospital, and that they needed on-call flexible nurses to fill in especially during summer and Christmas for vacations. Now I could not accept another position such as resource nurse on a permanent basis because I would be removed from the laid off list for the Mother-Baby Unit. I was hoping a position would come available as I was the most senior of our six laid off nurses.

As the clinic director and I met the next day, she found that the hospital's contract for allowing laid-off nurses to work in the clinic was clear-cut. We were to be offered shifts there also. This was a great opportunity because I could see a woman in the clinic for her prenatal visits and follow her after she delivered her baby on the Mother-Baby Unit. I worked in specialty areas such as the diabetes clinic for pregnant women and genecology clinic for those who were not.

It was less than a month before my own unit was competing with the clinic to have me fill shifts. I never once missed one of my boy's sporting events, as all my evenings were free. I did not have to work as many weekends and did so only when the kids needed something extra.

I was on the layoff list for almost one year. A 50% evening position became available and so I had to take it. My youngest was about to graduate from high school and I was able to find work for him and his brother in the logistics department at the hospital on evening shifts. Two years later a full-time day shift position became available, and as my two young men, and their younger sisters found their wings, mom was back to her normal routine.

Heavenly Father had blessed our family in so many ways. Not once during that year of lay-off did any of my children have a medical bill that I could not handle. I was able to increase my knowledge as I worked in areas of women's cancer treatment, prenatal care, and gynecology, something that would not have happened without being pushed to look for shifts in other areas of the hospital. The most important lesson that I learned though was how merciful God is. So often He knows what is possible or what might lie ahead. He is always near to help us. Sometimes it is up to us to take that leap of faith when we feel His presence near. It is up to us to have faith when that still small voice whispers and says, *"Please be still and know I am here."*

Some of My Best Friends

When I was a little girl, it was sometimes difficult having a sister who had a disability. Back then, of course, my world revolved around me. Sometimes I questioned God and asked Him why I had to have a pest for a little brother and a "blind girl" for a sister. I hated that she was different. I hated how people made fun of her everywhere we went. I did not understand then what I would come to realize later. God knew exactly what he was doing. He knew I needed to learn about love and patience.

Those years of tolerating others' behaviors and learning to give limitless service would, as time passed, mold me into the person I was to become. "Those" people that others were sure to shy away from would ultimately become some of my best friends.

I have seen for myself the beauty of a disabled person, especially those whose intellect sets them apart from others. They have no guile. They place no judgments. My niece Jessica was a perfect example of this.

My granddaughter Emma is disabled. She speaks only a few words. And, I cannot think of a sweeter way to receive a kiss. When you ask, "Can I have a kiss, Emma?" she does not pucker her lips. She instead opens her mouth wide and rubs her mouth against your cheek as she quickly runs by. But really, it is a kiss.

Another example was a young man whose mother had been kicked and abused repeatedly when he was still in her womb. I went to visit him with his brother at a state hospital where he resided. He was so excited to see his brother Bruce. The first thing he did was to run over to his dresser and retrieve his picture of Jesus. And Hugs! We received one hug after another. He was a conduit directly from Heaven, to be sure.

Many of my dancing friends warned me it would be unwise to befriend "Tommy." I did not listen. I met him for a steak dinner—always my treat—at a popular dance club in Portland. He could not master the waltz, but he was asked on many occasions to teach others his version of the cha-cha. It was magnificent. We rarely danced slow dances, but when we did, he sang the words loudly as a serenade, and his spit would sometimes hit my cheeks. Tommy had cerebral palsy. One night I went dancing even though I had had the most miserable day at work. I was tired and sad, and my spirit was low.

Tommy suddenly stopped his serenade, looked me in the eye and proclaimed, "God wants me to tell you how much he loves you, Kim."

God knew how much I needed to hear those words that day, so he said them through Tommy.

My friend Maggie cares for five mentally challenged adults in her home. One time one of them was hospitalized. Maggie and her brood were all together in the hospital room visiting Dixie. I found unopened celery and carrots with dip in the refrigerator, passed over by a discharged diabetic patient, and gave it to them. They made it a picnic and were happy and appreciative when I left the room.

Randy is my favorite. He is Maggie's nephew. Randy's mother had cancer. She would not terminate her pregnancy. The uterine tumor pressed on one side of Randy's skull, so his brain could not develop correctly. He is in his sixties. I love his smile. I love his kindness. He loves my frosted sugar cookies. He hides them under his bed, so Dixie doesn't eat them all. He recently shared the following story:

"Ya know, Kim. Ya know what the doctor said when I was born?" said Randy.

"No, I don't, Randy."

"He said I'd never live to be three-days-old! Ya know, Kim? Ya know what he said when I was six?"

"No Randy. What did he say?"

"He said I would never grow up! That's what he said, Kim. And guess what? Guess what, Kim? I'm still living, and the DOCTOR is the one who is dead!"

My husband and I laughed so hard our sides hurt. I almost wet myself. It wouldn't have mattered though for I was in the company of some of my very best friends.

Unto the Least of These

Please don't judge me by my cover,
for I know just what you'll see,
All the Earthly imperfections
that our Father gave to me.

You'll only see my crippled shape;
perhaps, the fact I cannot see.
Or you might find I do not hear
the words you speak to me.

Perhaps I am unruly or sing
loudly for it's all I know,
Maybe I can't understand,
because my mind is slow.

Or if loud noises scare me
and set my mind into a whirl,
Please, take another look at me;
please step into my world.

For if you have a loving heart, you'll
find there's more to me.

To Know He Is There

My soul is just the same as yours and
it senses who loves me.

People say "It's such a shame"
and pass by my loving heart;
afraid to care, afraid to touch,
so afraid to give one part.

But they should ask my family
and those who care for me.
They would say "The shame's in them,
who have not hearts, indeed."

For I was sent here just for them,
to teach them a greater love;
a little glimpse of Heaven and how things
work up above.

It never was by accident, that my cover
was Earthly frail.
Father blessed my family here
to live much closer to the veil.

And when I am departed;
when all days come to an end
I'll run into the loving arms
of my family; my truest friends.

For their eyes did not see limits in the
Person I could be.
They felt my soul, reached out their hands
and looked beyond what others see.

For with kind hearts,
they did it unto Him,
because, I...was the "least of these"

Dedicated to my Family
2015

The Blessing

Sara was just simply *not* the Sara that I had come to know. As I walked into her room that morning, I was not greeted with her warming smile and cheerful countenance. That day, she seemed withdrawn and fatigued. Anxiety had replaced the calm. Worry was pressed into the lines of her forehead.

"I just can't do this another day, Kim!" Sara said. "The room is closing in on me and the bed sheets are making me itch all over. I just cannot do this for another three weeks. Please, Kim, call the doctor. I need him to release me to go home."

Her words caught me so off-guard. All her nurses had worried that this day might come. We all knew that if Sara left too soon, her sons would not survive. We had all marveled at her strength. She had never complained, not once. I had been her Primary Nurse for nearly three months—three long months—with the head of her bed being tilted downward at a 30-degree angle. She was allowed only a few minutes each day to shower and move about, and then it was right back to bed. Her womb carried precious cargo, two premature twin boys who were too anxious to make their appearance. These two little ones needed time for their lungs to mature. It had taken great inner strength for Sara to put aside her own needs. Her world existed from the surroundings of her bed. Only the phone and the television kept her in touch with what took place outside her four hospital walls.

I felt her stress. She had persevered long past the time that most of us would have quit. She was beyond those words,

"Sara, you can do this." I felt so frustrated because my mortal self could no longer bring her encouragement. I paused for a long moment and tried to rally all my thoughts. And then it just came out, out of nowhere! Like a thump on the back.

"Sara," I paused. "If you were a member of my church, I would know exactly what to do for you. You need a blessing."

She cared so much for these little ones that she wanted to know more. "What is a blessing," she asked, and so we talked.

I told her about the Priesthood. I told her about my first remembered blessing when I had the measles and my fever would not break. I told her how I felt when loving hands were placed upon my head and the deep sleep I fell into. I could see her interest was genuine as we talked but I did not want to push.

I asked, "Sara, do you belong to a church?" Her answer was no. She and her husband did not attend any services.

"What about your family."

"No," she said again. "No one was much of a churchgoer," she went on, except for her brother. "It was really interesting, Kim," she shared. "A few years ago, when my brother was in high school, he was getting into a lot of trouble, drinking, and all the things kids can do. But then he met a group of kids at school and he got so involved with their church that he stopped all mischief, even cussing. To this day, he won't take a drink. My husband and I sometimes watch my brother's little boy. Well, that is, we used to, until I had to be in the hospital. My brother and his wife go to this building once a month. I think they call it a Temple or something. Perhaps you've seen it, Kim. You can see it from the freeway in Southwest Portland. It has an, oh, it looks like an ang—"

"An angel!" I finished. "Yes, it's a gold angel and he is blowing a horn. A Horn, Sara, a Horn!" My heart almost stopped. "Please, Sara, call your brother! Ask him to give you a blessing."

And so, she did. I was not able to be there as I was to start my vacation the next day, and...I will never know the blessings that were promised to her. I was thrilled, upon my return to learn that she had remained for three more weeks.

We all wondered if we would ever see Sara again as we knew she was to have her babies at a hospital nearer to her home. I was coming out of the medication room one day a few weeks later and there, to everyone's joy, was Sara. A baby son tucked lovingly into each arm. I watched from a distance, sharing in all her amazing joy, thinking back on those long, difficult months.

"What a miracle it was," she shared, as she told everyone how she carried the babies past their due date.

My heart was so full. And then Sara's eyes caught mine. She placed each baby into nurses' arms and came towards me.

As we shared the embrace, she whispered in my ear, "Thank you so much for my blessing."

I hugged her tightly. "Heavenly Father loves you so much," I whispered back.

As Sara left that day, the other nurses wanted to know what was whispered in my ear. Some things, however, are just too tender to be shared.

A Most Amazing Conference Call

One year at Christmas time, my husband and I were given the name of a woman in our congregation that might need a little help. Names were never hard to come by. This, however, would be the first year that we met with great difficulty in delivering our Christmas gift to them.

The woman we had chosen lived only two miles down the road from us, which turned out to be a blessing, for try as we might, we could not get her to answer her door. This sweet lady had lost her husband that year, so we understood she might be leery of strangers. Along with knocking on her door in the early evening, we tried stopping at her house during the day. A red car was usually parked in her driveway, but still, no answer to our knocking. We wondered if she was gone for the holidays and then tried to call her. The phone just kept on ringing. We then called the person who gave us her name. We learned that this sister had become quite guarded since her husband's passing. We were given the name of the couple in our congregation who were supplying her with wood to heat her home. They said she was not out of town.

I tried a few more times as I headed off to the bank or to the grocery store. Each time the result was the same. The woodpile however was changed, and her car was home one time and not the next. I really thought she was home. I really wanted her to have our gift, but I finally took the box out of my car and put it away but not out of sight. I did not want it to be forgotten.

The days passed, one by one, bringing Christmas ever so near. I started thinking about who else might need the package's contents, and even though a name would come to mind, a reason was soon found to think back on this woman. It would be her first Christmas without her sweetheart. I kept thinking about all the memories that Christmas brings and all the thoughts about family. My heart was heavy. Perhaps, I thought, I've been calling the wrong person. I went to my bedroom and set the Christmas box on my bed. I dropped to my knees and decided to call home. There was only one person who knew where that box needed to go. I placed it back into my car. I then went to finish last minute Christmas details in town. I turned right at our stop sign, never thinking to turn left for one last try. I was going to find someone who needed our gift. I had only traveled a few blocks and was strongly prompted to turn around. I tried to convince myself that the feeling was only because I had tried so many times before and that I needed to try once more. I ignored the prompting and continued on my course. The further I traveled, the more despairing I felt. I pulled abruptly over and turned quickly around. Never once in those moments did I wonder if she would be home. It was time to go there, now.

I pulled into her familiar driveway, and much to my surprise, I could see a little lady as I walked up to the back door. I motioned for her to open the door and showed her the package from outside. She cautiously opened the door.

"Are you Mrs. Thornton?" I asked. As I told her that it had been quite a quest to make my delivery, she simply looked at me in wonder. "It must be difficult for you this year," I said as I handed her the box. "Perhaps you can use the money for something you need. Maybe to pay a bill or buy yourself something you've been wanting."

Her eyes began to tear. We shared a hug and she told me how she "just needed some time and she would be back to church again." I expressed my love. She expressed her gratitude.

When my husband and I went to church the Sunday after Christmas, we learned how special that day really was for her and for me. The couple who delivered wood to her told us how Mrs. Thornton expressed to them how sad she had been. Having lost her husband and having nothing at all for Christmas, she and I both had been on our knees that morning. She asked that someone might care. I asked "who" needed our care. Once we both phoned home, God's angels took over from there. I like to remember it as—A most amazing conference call.

Little Birds

I love birds. I love to open the door to our backyard and hear their soft chirping. If you listen intently, you can enjoy how they communicate one to another. I listen in awe to the elaborate signals that float from tree to tree, telling about food,

To Know He Is There

danger, and of their needs. Yes, especially of their needs and how softly and quietly they take care of their little community nestled high within our trees.

Esme was extremely sick fighting two types of deadly lymphoma. She was weak and weary battling to save her life. For every few steps she took forward on her journey to save her life, set-backs followed, leaving her without the resources, both physical and temporal, to fight back. Bills were mounting and food was scarce. She had many things to accomplish before she could go for further cancer treatment 250 miles away. Each one required more money and greater strength—the two things that for her seemed to be fading away quickly.

What Esme did not know was that a "little bird" who knew of her great needs had softly chirped into the ear of another little bird. So gentle was the sound, so quiet the request, but it was heard.

The one little bird did not know Esme, only that she had been an employee at the hospital where Little Bird also worked. This is what she remembers about November 26, the Sunday after Thanksgiving...

I drove to the address I was given for Esme's house. I was on my way to church. There was a truck parked outside. Everything seemed quiet. No blinds were opened. My thought was that perhaps they were gone for the holiday weekend. I was disappointed and went on to church. I drove by the house again after church and everything was the same.

It was a dreary Sunday, no sunshine to be seen. I had prepared some things for Esme. I found the most incredible fleece blanket material with little white daisies on a pink background with the cancer emblem on it for her to have in the hospital. I trimmed it with a rose color binding. I selected a few homemade jellies I thought she might like. I could not leave the package on her doorstep to be stolen as there was one more important gift in the basket to be given.

It felt awkward to knock on the door of a complete stranger but my cold knuckles did so anyway. There was no answer. I was prompted to knock harder when I heard a voice inside. A slender young lady answered the door. Her head was covered with a wrap. I asked if she was Esme. She came outside. It was obvious that she was terribly ill. Her affect was soft as well as her voice. I told her that I heard she needed help. I told her that many years ago I, too, needed help just after Thanksgiving Day. I expressed to her how I felt when my hope was dwindling as I struggled so hard. I then told her that some of the quarters had rolled under the jellies when I tried to put the lid on the money jar. She looked up at me. Her tear-filled eyes expressed her gratitude. My tear-filled eyes expressed my joy. I did not give her my name. My love seemed enough. I know it was gently raining when I went back to my car, but the day seemed so much brighter even though there was still no sun.

Esme wrote on Facebook to her friends on November 26. "Sunday was a bad day for me. I woke from horrible dreams filled with fear and doubt. I tried to get my mind off of it, but I felt helpless and in the 'doldrums.' Then Sunday evening there was knock on my door. I went to the door and an Angel handed me back my hope."

The next day when I returned to work, yet another little bird told me that Esme wanted to know my name, as she was searching to find out who I was. My name did not matter. That this little bird told me how excited Esme and her family were to go to the grocery store and have gas money—well, that is what mattered. "Chirp, Chirp."

~ ~ ~

Little birds chirped of Esme's progress throughout the coming year, as did she on Facebook. She was conquering her great battle with lymphoma. She was hopeful, and her countenance became cheerful. *Why then*, I thought, *do I feel so strongly that this little bird needs help?*

It was Christmas Eve, the following year, and a prompting to help Esme would not be quiet. So many thoughts went through my mind. Does she need help to buy Christmas gifts? Does she have enough food? Stores would close for Christmas soon.

Her husband Andrew answered the knock on their door. I placed a gift into his hand. "Who are you?" he asked.

I ran to my car, but Esme's sweet voice could be heard from a distance. "You are a coward! Come back and give me a hug."

We ran to each other to embrace.

I worked Christmas day, as nurses sometimes must. Mid-afternoon, I received a most wonderful Christmas present. There at my nurse's station stood Andrew and Esme with a beautiful card and a little hand-made origami bird. It was Esme's Christmas gift to me, a beautiful gift from her heart.

"Thank you for letting us be warm this Christmas," she softly whispered.

I was so thankful that God had spoken to my soul for He knew Esme's house would need heat for the winter, a sad and heartbreaking winter. This bird, so eager to be cancer free and to fly once more, was given the news that she most likely would not live to see summer. Her little body had once again been taken hostage by her worst enemy—lymphoma.

So many little birds heard of her needs. So many little birds gave her care. So many little birds shared fond memories with and about Esme, while they could. Cherished by family and surrounded by friends, she was wrapped in the arms of love. Little Bird took her final breath on a sad March morning.

Now freed from your destroyer, go and soar so high. Oh, Little Bird! Little Bird! Fly away home.

Little Bird, perched in my heart, how did you come to fly there?
The skies abound, yet, your need was found, chirped quietly into my ear.
Oh, Little Bird, your needs were great, but our Father's love much greater.
He touched my soul, said quietly, "Go, go now, you'll know why later."
Oh, Little Bird, was I too late to get to know you better?

My heart grows sad as you slip away, and I can only sit here.
"Oh, must you go? No, not today." My heart is almost breaking,
Then be freed from the bondage that binds your wings,
And fly, fly away!

For Our Esme

A Time and a Season

I can remember that Christmas so clearly. It was 1983. I had not celebrated Christmas since my divorce a few months earlier. I was just beginning my first year of nursing school. I had six children, five of them under ten years of age.

The Portland mornings were becoming wet and cold as I contemplated what Christmas would be like that year. We were struggling. It was faith and prayer that took care of any extra expenses beyond our meager and tight budget. I was renting a house that was small and humble. Money was in short supply while stress came in abundance. As I looked over our bills, I saw no money for Christmas. By cutting way back on the food budget and with the money I would not need for gas because of the Christmas break, I was able to manage one small gift for each child.

The thought came to me often, how poor children must feel at Christmas time. How does a struggling mother tell her little ones that Santa could not come? Our focus was so wrong, for Christmas was a celebration of our Savior, not of Santa.

On Christmas Eve there was a knock on our door. Some leaders from our church were there, standing on our porch, with bright smiles on their faces and gifts in their arms. My children were so excited. I was overwhelmed as tears rushed to my eyes. I was hurt and confused as I stood there and realized that I felt angry that I could not provide on my own.

I cannot to this day remember the name of the leader of our women's group, but I do remember how she wrapped me in her arms and whispered to me.

"Kim, it is always harder to receive that it is to give. Remember this day and when you become a nurse, you will be able to give. There is a time and a season for everything."

I have thought of her words so many times. Years later I cherished the truth in them.

How our lives changed from that Christmas on. Were we ever richer for the things on the earth? Not with a family of seven. The next year we decided unanimously to anonymously spread joy during the Christmas season. It became our focus to find a friend or family member that we could share our hearts with. We all realized that it was impossible to feel sad or alone when we let Christ be the focus of Christmas. One year we chose an elderly lady who lived across the street in a nursing home. We visited her all year long. Our commitment to her turned into a loving and lasting friendship. It was great fun. Each child would try to "Pixie" a home without getting caught. Homemade gifts and cookies were left on many doorsteps over the years.

As for me, I did become a nurse. Heavenly Father continues to prompt me through the wonderful gift of the Holy Ghost to know who is in need of a prayer, a gift of time and sometimes even the gift of the gospel.

I cannot close this story without telling you how true my leader's words became. There was a time and a season. Many years later when I was at work, I stepped into our lounge where one of our aides was taking her break. She was talking with the power company on the phone, pleading with them to keep her power on. She too had six children to raise on her own. How the tears came to her eyes as she told me her story there in the break room. She had prayed to Heavenly Father the night before and asked him to please not let her family be cold on Christmas day, especially not during their celebration of the Savior's birth. She told of how she and her little ones were going to sing songs together and then share homemade gifts with one another.

All the nurses on the Family Birth Center had full hearts that day. They emptied their pocketbooks and all stuck to the same story and a vow never to tell her our version of the "Miracle." Our aide was always to believe that a pretty, blonde woman had come to our unit with that envelope full of money. It was a gift from this woman, a gift for our aide who took such good care of her when she had her baby there. Each nurse described our phantom lady in the same way, with the same detail, right down to the color of her shoes. Have I since repented for that sin of telling a lie? Well, maybe.

Her house was warm that Christmas and would be for many months to come. I know our hearts were all warmer because, as someone once said, "There is a time and a season."

It was our time and most definitely the season.

How Did You Know?

Wonderful things can happen to you when you go grocery shopping. I go two times a month to shop at WinCo Foods. I travel 30 miles away from my home to get there, just to save money. My husband thinks I'm crazy. I know that I am not, for each time I return home, I always have a story to share with him.

Selecting the groceries that go into my cart—well that is tedious. Putting them all onto the conveyer belt—well that takes little skill. Packing them myself, quickly, so the next person in line doesn't have to wait—a bit more exciting. Then as my bags are loaded, teetering precariously, one on top of one another—well now, that is when my fun at the WinCo store can begin.

To Know He Is There

You see, my grocery budget includes a $20 tip to the person the Lord wants it to go to, to the person who will load my groceries into my car. I pray about the bill's recipient before I ever leave home. I search for its recipient the moment I am ready to load my groceries into my car. I am always successful because the Lord knows who is in need.

On this particular summer afternoon, I was going to return home, not only with a story to tell, but with my heart so full, my loaded car was of no comparison.

I looked intently, as I always did for that "special someone" and really was having trouble feeling inspired. I could not find my "helper" for he was not near the bagging area but instead, sitting on a bench, located near the entry way, just before people left the store. He was ever so patiently sitting there, with his own bag of groceries in his lap.

I knew that he was the one. I felt both excited and relieved.

"Hey," I said. "Would you like to earn some money?" His eyes lit up, but soon he hesitated. "It's legal," I smiled. "All you have to do is put my groceries in my car. Twenty dollars you earn," I told him, "and this nurse's back is saved."

As we walked to my car, I couldn't help but notice the winding scars he had on his nearly shaven head. I thought to myself how he must have been in a terrible accident or had major injury to have such scars. He was cheerful, and it was easy to see that he was happy to be of service. He was kind and careful to pack each bag just so. He was loading the last bag into my trunk when I reached into my purse on the front seat of my car. As I went to grasp the $20, a feeling rushed over me, and, in **no uncertain terms**, the Lord told me "Give him all that you have."

"Really, Heavenly Father?" I questioned, for I had just cashed my paycheck. My concern evaporated quickly, and I took out all the bills to be found in the wallet.

I put the money in the young man's hand.

"This was not our agreement," he said softly.

"Heavenly Father told me you need this," I argued.

He did not let go of my hand but used it to pull me closer

to him. He held me close for a long time. When he released his hug, I could see the tears in his eyes.

"How did you know?" he questioned.

I was confused, and stated "How did I know what?"

His story then unfolded. He had battled cancer for months. An ugly tumor had relentlessly returned, requiring him to have many surgeries.

"I am dying," he said quietly. "I want to be independent for as long as I am able. I have had so many medical expenses that I could not pay my electric bill. My friend brings me to the store, so I can buy food each day. How on earth did you know?" he said as he started to weep, "This is the exact amount I need to turn my electricity back on. My friend will be here soon to pick me up. Can you please wait to meet him?"

We hugged for the second time, the last time. It was I who could not let go. We both felt the warm embrace of Father's love. I could not stay for my groceries would not keep in the warm summer day. The sun's rays, however, could not compare to the glow I felt in my heart as I slowly waved good-bye—for the very last time.

Stressful Bliss

My life changed forever the day I smiled at Mike. I don't mean a physical smile. I mean one of those yellow smiley faces you post on "L.D.S. Mingle." He didn't smile back right away, but I did not care for I had some 260 e-mails to respond to on my newly established "Mingle" account.

I found out about the dating site only a few days before I sent Mike a smile. I found out about him weeks later when he posted a reply. Smiles turned into a phone call. The phone call later turned into a date. Each date was a 240-mile commute for one of us. Months later we became a blended family with 14 children, 12 still living and one who would not live long if we could not rein her in a bit.

No words could describe our new situation better than "stressful bliss." Months would pass, and words would fly as we tried to find common ground to keep us anchored. One night, Mike and I had a terrible quarrel about one of the children. Mike stormed out, leaving me with harsh words and said he was going an hour away to help fix his parent's computer. Hours went by and Mike did not return home.

When I called his parents with concern, they said he left their home hours ago. Because of our quarrel, I thought perhaps he did not want to come home at all. By midnight I felt that something was terribly wrong. I knelt on my knees for an answer. The answer came quickly as I telephoned hospitals in the outlying areas.

Mike had been rear-ended by a drunk driver. His head had broken the rear cab window of his truck from the impact of another truck. He had a severe concussion that would leave him dizzy and nauseated for months to come. His stitched incision would shed glass for years. I asked the nurse if Mike even wanted to see me again.

She answered, "Of course your husband wants to see you." Her words were "stressful bliss."

My life should calm down now that I have remarried, I thought to myself. That thought was to be in error. We had just settled with our insurance company after months of head spinning and nausea for Mike.

Dr. Chua, upon overhearing a conversation about my sweetie, quickly stated, "I know exactly what is wrong with your husband. He has knocked the crystals loose in his inner ear."

He was right. Soon life was better but for only a while.

It was almost one year later when life would tip us upside down once more. Our new primary care doctor asked us if there were any health concerns we had about Mike as we were in his office establishing care. I was quick to speak up—not necessarily one of my virtues, mind you—but that day, it was a Godsend.

"I don't mind that my husband has a goiter in his neck but has anyone tried to see what is inside of it?" I asked.

Later at work, I had just put the phone down when I was told I had a call from my husband.

"I have cancer," Mike said. "The biopsy showed stage three thyroid cancer."

My supervisor at work told me I could go home early. I chose, however, to use the time to find one of our hospital's best surgeons, Dr. James. Dr. James said he would be coming back from his break the day after Christmas.

"How about we do Mike's surgery the day after I return, Kim?" he said.

I couldn't believe my ears. He was so kind. His voice was reassuring. Mike and I soon found out why. We went to Dr. James's office for a pre-surgery visit. As soon as we sat down, I noticed a painting on the wall. There standing around a patient undergoing surgery was the surgical team. Standing next to the surgeon was the Lord speaking into his ear, guiding him through surgery.

Mike's planned three-hour surgery was nearly twice as long. I sat in the surgical waiting room with that picture foremost in my mind. I knew Heavenly Father was there for my husband. I knew he was also there for Dr. James. Radiation would soon follow.

A suspicious area appeared on a PET scan a year later. More radiation would follow. He was glowing during those days after radiation—and I do mean literally—and kids, grandkids, puppy and I all had to keep our distance.

That was over a decade ago. Today, well now, our family has grown. We have moved from that big old house. Even though Mike and I downsized, our family has not. We have over 30 grandchildren that make our house a home, a home full of "stressful bliss."

5 RAYS OF SUNSHINE THROUGH THE STORM

Life can be so difficult at times. Like the darkest storm clouds overhead, life can sometimes pull you into gloomy places. Sometimes life's storms can bring intense winds, making you uncertain of your footing. There are times when life's storms bring pounding rain that makes you run for cover. Then when you think you can withstand no more, you will see those rays of sunshine pushing through the clouds. It can start with someone's smile. Sometimes those rays push through, changing the most challenging day into calmness, the saddest days into hopeful ones, or a day that you will long remember. May the rays of sunshine and laughter be there for you at the end of your most stormy day.

The Not-So-Innocent

It has been 30 years now that I have been a Registered

Nurse. I could write a book about the incredibly humorous situations nurses find themselves in. I also look back to the time when I first realized that nurses themselves sometimes have hands ready for fun.

In 1989 I accepted a position on the Mother-Baby Unit of a renowned, Portland, Oregon hospital. Two of the nurses on the unit possessed an abundance of humor. Their names were Heidi and Danielle.

I remember that crisp winter day. Heidi was dressing a baby on the procedure table in the newborn holding room. The 15 by 15 area doubled as our nursery. Having dressed and swaddled a baby and with its beanie in place, Heidi motioned for Danielle passing by in the hall.

"Hey, Danielle, could you hold my baby? Just for a moment," Heidi said.

Without warning or Danielle's reply, Heidi threw the pass. The tiny bundle traveled midair, nearly 15 feet! Danielle lunged forward in panic as an adrenalin rush stabbed her heart! She caught and embraced the baby, the rather hard baby, the cute little C.P.R. mannequin. Quietly and without any to do, Danielle placed the doll on the nearby counter.

Firmly and succinctly, she proclaimed. "I would not be turning your back for one moment if I were you!"

Months passed by with only a small prank here and there. And then, one mid-summer morning, it happened...

Our unit was busy and almost all of our beds were occupied. The holding room cradled bassinets side-by-side. One baby's cry set off an entire choir.

Newly delivered Mrs. Zouch-Keeney, listed on our board as occupying room 27, had a note placed on the outside of her door. "Please do not disturb until after eight a.m." Danielle was quick to let Heidi know that this mother's baby would need to room-in sooner. He was wailing and hungry now!

Heidi entered the nursery and began examining crib name cards. There he was. Danielle stayed nearby, lurking near the nursery's entrance.

And then: the most blood curdling scream was heard well

above those already crying. Heidi looked closer at the crib card. It read, Baby boy Zouch-Keeney. Weight: 8 pounds, 6 ounces. Length: 18 inches. And indeed, it was. It was a swaddled 8-pound 6-ounce zucchini!!

"Danielle! Danielle! Where are you? You! You...are Soooooooo DEAD!"

> Author's note: All names in this story have been changed to protect the not-so-innocent!

Florence Nightingale

I remember my most humorous nursing situation. It happened to me long before my name tag had the letters R.N. added to it. I was an aide-in-training and had not yet graced any hospital floor with my presence.

My friend Ed suggested we visit our recovering friend and fellow church member one evening. Heart be still, a chance to see Dan! Dan was tall, dark and handsome. (Did I mention available?) I could see me now, Florence Nightingale, holding Prince Charming's hand, empathy going unleashed for the betterment of mankind, especially This man kind.

Ed and I entered Dan's room. A dressing hugged Dan's chest from Adam's apple to navel. Staples securing the incision ran the distance. He was thrilled to have visitors, yet dubious in the comfort of Ed being one of them. Ed radiated unrestrained humor. Once in Ed's company, jokes would fly and sides would ache from laughter. The "Promise" was made that Ed would not make Dan laugh, and so the focus of conversation touched on pain pills and cute nurses.

I was in awe at the magnitude of Dan's suffering. I reduced myself to a shy visitor, listening quietly. And then it happened.

It was the moment to prove my compassion, a chance to embark in the direction of my praiseworthy career!

"Kim," Dan petitioned, "could you please get me some water?"

Here was my moment! I, Florence Nightingale, was to quench the thirst of one battle scarred man. My heart raced wildly.

I grabbed his water pitcher. "I'll be right back, uh, oh, I'll be only a moment," I stammered.

Their conversation hushed to a still silence as I neared the exit to go to the unit's kitchen. It first began with Ed. It was that laugh. It was unmistakable! It had only one owner. It was piercing, like that of an ambulance siren.

Dan's laugh quickly followed. "Kim! Oh, Kim! Make him stop! Ouch, oh, Ouch!"

But laugh they did until tears stained their cheeks and Dan could laugh no more.

Disturbed and angry, I snarled. Then, losing all Sainthood, I shouted, "What in Heaven's name is so funny?"

Being quiet for a moment (and mind you the briefest moment), Ed with every ounce of composure that he could muster, stumbled, "Kim, umm, do you know what you are carrying in your hand?"

Then Prince Charming, eager to rub salt into my gaping wound, taunted, "Nurse, oh Nurse, please, I need more pain pills!"

Today, my name tag reads Kimberly R.N. and it should be of no surprise that this Florence Nightingale NEVER mistook a patient's urinal for a water pitcher again!

Nettie Jones

Nettie jones was a special patient. The time spent with her was no more than a day. The impression she left in my heart will last a lifetime.

Two years into my nursing career, I accepted a temporary float assignment at Providence Hospital. I was thrilled to have my little white nursing shoes planted on the same unit for a full six weeks.

I wore my soft white belted dress that day. My long hair actually relented and fell into perfect curls. Even my mood was in rare form as I arrived early to receive that day's assignment.

All the day shift nurses listened to the night-shift's report. Everyone listened to the words on the tape recorder, but I know they hit me harder than anyone else in the room, for she was to be my patient.

"Do not be surprised if Mrs. Jones has already passed away by the time you make your morning rounds."

Suddenly, I was worried. I had not witnessed a death. What would I do for her as a mere human being? What would be my responsibilities as her nurse?

I disobeyed my most innate nursing judgment and assessed my least critical patients first. With that being accomplished and with grave trepidation, I knocked on Mrs. Jones' door. There was no answer. I knocked once more. All was silent. There were no stirrings to be heard from her room. I entered. The room was dark, with only the light from the hall showing the silhouette of her existence in the background. I moved closer, slowly, and fearful at what I might find. I heard no breathing. My hand trembled as it reached over the top of her head for the chain that dangled from her overhead light. In what seemed to be an eternal moment, I glanced downward. Her closed eyes flew open and my poor heart nearly stopped.

"Lordie, Lordie!" she cried. "I have died and gone to heaven. And the most beautiful angel has come to take me home."

My heart sighed with relief as she lovingly looked upon my face. I was deeply touched by her comment. In that brief moment, my dilemma was now reversed, for how was I to tell her she was still alive?

Never was I so sad to tell a patient, "Hello, I am your nurse for today."

Mrs. Jones did pass away later that same day. And you can be certain, the next Angel to greet her was by far prettier than me.

Mrs. Sullivan

When I was 19, I took a class at Portland Community College called Fitness and Conditioning. It was there that I was first introduced to Joan Sullivan. She was the instructor for most of the female fitness classes at the college. She was slender and tan. Her hair was light blonde. I had never met anyone with such enthusiasm. She would lead us in exercises and never sweat. She just glowed. It was embarrassing. How could anyone twice my age have twice my energy? Yet, she did.

"Raise those legs, girls, jump that rope. Girls, come on now! You can do it!"

Anyone who survived her class deserved an "A." To pass her final, you had to run five miles in less than a given time. Never was I so glad to be finished with a class. Never was I so tired after a class. Her class was worth every penny. Trimmer thighs and a lowered stress level were my reward.

When I was 33, mind you almost 15 years later, my fellow nursing students and I decided to shed our unwanted pounds before we walked across the stage at graduation. You tend to nibble as you study, and I guess you could say I studied a lot. So, we all decided to sign up for Body Conditioning 101. The four of us looked so glamorous in our leotards and tights. Head bands were in position and tennis shoes were double-tied as we entered the gym that day. We were full of pep, choosing to take the class in the morning to get us off to a good start for those three days of the week.

"Hello, ladies. So glad you could join me."

There she was, the same blonde hair, that same smile. Don't gym teachers ever die! She had to be at least 50. She had no belly. She still had Lana Turner's legs. Just bury me now! What had we done? Or should I say, what was going to be done to us? I had been the one to suggest we take the class in the morning. Big, I mean, BIG mistake! If we had taken the class in the afternoon we could have at least crawled to our cars. As it was, we would be gimping along every Monday, Wednesday, and Friday afternoons.

I was the mother of six kids. Do you know how silly it looks wearing an adult diaper under your leotard when you jump rope for 20 minutes?

"Circle those arms, ladies. Kick those legs now. Isn't this fun?" (Are we *supposed* to say, *yes, I'm having a ball, how about you?*) "Don't forget your Kegels, girls. Tighten those glutes."

She was going to reduce my Gluteus Maximus into a Gluteus Minimus in no time at all. We worked hard. We laughed, we sweat and some days we cried. I mean, we were so sore we actually cried.

It was amazing. It was one term before graduation and our studying was non-stop, but we did not dare nibble too much at night when we knew we had to work out so hard on those following mornings. Our reward was noticeable. Each one of us was able to be at least one dress size smaller on graduation evening and not one of us was panting as we hiked the stairs to cross the stage.

That was a long time ago. I am afraid to take another fitness class at the college. I hear old gym instructors never die; they just roll over.

"Now roll to the right and one and two…then roll to the left, now three and four…"

6 NOT WITHOUT MY CHILDREN

I have made my share of mistakes while here in this mortal existence; having six children was not one of them. Were we poor? To be sure. Were we blessed? Always. My children, all with children of their own now, look back on those times and tell me being poor helped to make them the adults they are today. Their ethics and integrity are rooted deeply with the slogan, "If you want something, go out and work for it." My grandmothers were no strangers to hardship and their stories helped me to never quit. I too had burdens to bear, but I would never have climbed so high, not without my children.

Forced Family Fun

My little chicks left home just as close together as they entered it. Five little "stair steps" —as people would call them—were born within the space of six years. I had a glimpse of what separation would be like when their older brother

Tony passed away. It was incredibly difficult. I learned to cherish my children even more and hold tight to those special moments we had together. I knew they would all eventually "spread their wings."

B.J. (short for Bjarne) was my youngest and last to leave home. One day we were riding together in the car. I cannot remember where we were going, but B. J. and I will always remember the major delay we had on the freeway. It was not your normal traffic jam we came upon. You know, the ones with cars bumper-to-bumper, crawling at a snail's pace?

I had to brake suddenly when we saw the traffic jam ahead. It was a yellow parade of feathers. Mama Duckling was marching 13 babies, in a beautifully formed line across the freeway. There was one big problem she did not consider. All she knew was she could see a rain-made pond on the other side. There was, however, a 3-foot high cement partition running the length of the freeway separating the two–way lanes.

Looking into my rearview mirror I could see that there was enough time to push on the hazard lights. I had a box in the back seat. I quickly grabbed it and ran for the ducklings. Mama duck became stressed and flew off to the side of the freeway. When cars approached, they saw the ducklings' plight, and kept traffic paused while B.J. and I scooped up the little yellow fur balls.

We thought our task would be easy. Forget that thinking! Just as we got one duckling into the box, another one would soon climb out, for the box had no lid. The babies were scattering. I had nothing to cover the top of the box, not a coat, not a thing. I ran to the car and rolled down a back window. B.J. and I then put one baby in each hand and placed them on the back seat. Mind you, we were getting pecked on and pooped on by 13 not-so-happy babies.

They were now off the freeway and safely into the car. And, oh, could those little critters find their way around the inside of the car, from the back seat to the front. Opening the doors of the car soon presented a problem, for neither one of us could climb into the car without one of them trying to escape. People were kind to be so patient. I know they enjoyed our little performance of "Save the ducklings." So thankful we were NOT to be seen on the five o'clock news.

We had to get off the freeway and drive the back roads to get to "mama's" pond. We worried that she would not stay near when she realized her little marching procession was gone. We had to walk through the mud on that rainy Washington day to get to the pond. B.J. had taken off his shirt to cover our box full of babies. We looked pathetic. We didn't care. We were on a mission. Mama circled overhead. She could hear her babies' cries as we placed them one by one into the water. Mama would not come to them with us there. B.J. and I needed to leave the scene. It did not take long before she stopped circling the area and, we assume, landed next to her chicks.

We climbed back into the car with muddy shoes, wet hair, and duck droppings everywhere. What a team we were with a fond memory, to be sure.

My own little chick would leave home, not long past that day. He now has a little chick of his own. As for me, well, I have heart-felt memories, especially the one of halting traffic and saving the ducklings that were sure to make us have some "forced family fun."

A Lesson from the Rib Cruncher

Most times when a phone call came from my child's school, the conversation would begin with "Mrs. Knudson, I really need to speak with you." They really needed to speak with me, the weary mother of six little stair steps. That mother who had brought all six of them into this world with such varied and unique personalities. Oh, my! What a popular lady I was becoming. The first in the series of calls came only a week earlier.

"Mrs. Knudson! Are you aware that your son is selling his free lunch tickets to our students each morning before school starts?"

Of course I was mortified. One part of my brain was contemplating which punishment would be best, while another portion of my grey matter was wondering if this child would grow up to be a financial planner. A week did not even slip by before the second call came.

"Mrs. Knudson, your son keeps forgetting to turn in the proceeds from the school's Pepperoni Fund Raiser. Twenty-eight dollars to be exact."

What pepperoni sale? Which son? I have four to be exact. No doubt this son's proceeds were by now spent. I was becoming a bit concerned. Would I ever be able to raise six little ones on my own? With a feeling of anxiety rising and my self-esteem plummeting, I was in no mood for the third call.

"Mrs. Knudson? This is Buddy's teacher. I really need to speak with you."

How can three of four sons get into so much mischief in only one week I thought to myself. "Could you tell me what he has done?" I asked.

She really wanted to speak with me in person. "After school?" she asked.

Could Buddy's teacher possibly understand the dilemmas my mind would create in seven long hours? I was beyond worry. This was Buddy, my fourth-grade rib-cruncher. He was the little man that greeted me each day after work with "Mom, you look like you need a rib crunch!" Before I knew it, those nine-year-old arms were wrapped tightly around me, and CRUNCH! I was the recipient of a hug that told me that God had purposefully sent this little one to me.

Buddy came into this world self-assured. It was a gift. He was my gift. He had an amazing passion for life. He still does. He has such love for people. What could he have possibly done that warranted my presence at an unscheduled parent-teacher conference?

My nervous hand tapped meekly on Mrs. Smith's door at exactly three-thirty.

Her words were sweet. Her voice was gentle. "Something happened in our little classroom yesterday Mrs. Knudson. You needed to hear this in person. It is something I will not soon forget," she said with excitement.

And so the story soon unfolded. Buddy asked his teacher the day before if he could make an announcement to his class. He asked with such conviction that Mrs. Smith felt at ease in letting him do so. Buddy was a leader in his classroom. Chunky and blonde, and that day with purpose, he made his way to the front of the room.

"Hey Guys!" he announced, "I want to talk with you a minute."

Mrs. Smith said the room quickly grew silent. Buddy looked beyond his classmates as his eyes searched to the back of the room until he spotted Pedro. Pedro was the son of a poor migrant farm worker. He had been mainstreamed into Buddy's fourth grade class. His clothes were tattered and worn. He had been the recipient of cruel jokes and ridicule from the moment he entered Buddy's classroom that year.

"You all know Pedro," he said. Then with conviction he pronounced, "He is my friend!" Buddy looked straight at his teacher and asked, "Can Pedro move his desk next to mine?"

Startled and amazed at his request, Mrs. Smith stammered, "Of...uh...of course..."

Then my nine-year-old son placed one of his rib crunching arms squarely around the shoulders of this small forsaken boy. "I do not like the way you have been treating my friend!" and with a fist clenched in determination he warned, "If you treat him that way again you will have to answer to me!"

Pedro's desk was placed next to Buddy's within moments.

It was no surprise to me to learn at the final school parent-teacher conference that Pedro had taken his rightful place in the classroom with friends to remember from his fourth-grade year, but none so needed as his friend "The Rib-Cruncher."

Whatever

Kari came into my life during the early hours of a mid-June morning. Disrupting a sound and peaceful sleep, Kari set the tone for doing things her way. Peaceful sleep was illusive for months to come, but it did not matter, as I could not be weary as I held my sweet little baby tenderly in my arms. The nurses that first night referred to baby Kari as their "Little China Doll."

A full head of dark wavy hair covered her head. Her eyes were dark brown, and dimples could be seen in her cute little chipmunk cheeks. Those piercing brown eyes and sweet little smile would melt my heart on so many moments. They would be her defense when she knew full well that she was about to be scolded for being naughty. Though Kari had roll upon roll of dimpled fat, as some nursing babies do, she would toddle them away and soon earned the name "peanut." She was petite and shy. She rarely spoke and by 18 months of age our family was becoming concerned that her vocabulary was so small. Wasted worry that was, for she went from "mama" and "dada" to full sentences over-night. With a growing vocabulary, she conveyed her likes and dislikes, and rarely hesitated in doing so.

I remember how I purchased her first store-bought dress for Kari's third birthday. It was dashing, a yellow gingham dress with a striking white pinafore.

"I no like it. I no like it," she cried as we tried to get her to put it on.

She continued her protest until she finally outgrew it. She knew then as she knows now that yellow is not her color and never could be. There is too much olive tint to her beautiful skin.

Kari was a happy child. She was extremely bright and usually smiling. She was an organizer. That trait worked in her behalf, cooking in the kitchen, and helping with her younger brothers as she entered pubescence. But my, oh my, was it to be a thorn in my side as she entered those difficult teenage years. I had to stay one step ahead of her to keep her on the right path.

Occasionally there was a battle. I remember once when she was about 13. She had asked me about going to the movies with her friend. I did not approve of the movie she was begging to see, and just because "all my friends are going" did not make me relent. A week after asking about the movie, she wanted permission to spend the night with the same friend. I said yes but told her to be home by noon the next day. Noon came and noon passed. I called the home of her friend. I was told, "The girls are at a movie."

They were smart to sit in the front row thinking, "No mom would walk all the way to the front to check things out."

So wrong, and so busted! Not only did I walk to the front, but I walked right in front of all those mischievous eighth graders.

"Kari, isn't that your mom?" her best friend questioned.

Now, I knelt in front of "Miss Deceitful" herself and told her that we could do this the easy way or hard way. She, being embarrassed in front of her friends, chose the hard way. Yelling and snipping up the entire isle, we not-so-quietly made our exit.

When asked why she would deliberately disobey me, the resounding words jumped out of her sweet little mouth as she snapped "Whatever!"

Oh, how I hated that word. Plastered on tee shirts and sweatshirts, it was the latest flippant word to be used by defiant teenagers.

Kari would live that afternoon to see another day. Years flew by and Kari came to know what having defiant teenagers was all about.

Kari seemed to thrive on stress. She was married and the mother of four when the word "whatever" took on an entirely different meaning. She called during her break to vent to her mother, the nurse. Kari worked as a unit secretary at a busy Denver hospital. She was especially frustrated that day as she observed the interactions between the nurses, the doctors, and the patients.

After listening to what sounded like some of my own difficult days, I told my daughter, "Do something about it. The only way you will know what a nurse goes through is to become one yourself. You can become 'whatever' you want to be."

She managed to care for a family, work her night job and study through it all. This mom could barely hold back the tears, to safely manage the stage stairs, and walk proudly to pin my daughter as a graduate nurse.

Kari now works in three different fields of nursing and has the ability to help to make ends meet and is ready for *whatever* comes her way.

Written with permission from my loving daughter Katie, so that others might know.

For Sammy

Katie is my third born and my first girl. She came into the world with light brown hair and those same little chipmunk cheeks that were inherited by all my children. It became apparent at an early age that Katie was shy except when she was with her brothers. Before she turned three, we came to know that Heavenly Father had given us a child who was full of faith and spirituality.

She was always the first to volunteer for the assignment of prayer on our Family Home Evening chart. Her prayers were sweet and pleading when a family member or pet was ailing. Katie was about to turn six when I realized just how much she believed in prayer and its miracles. Katie came along with me and another lady from our church, when we went to visit Sister Ottley.

Sister Ottley led the children's music on Sunday and Wednesday afternoons. She had a beautiful voice and all of the children loved her dearly. Sister Ottley had developed a condition which required surgery on her vocal cords and was only able to speak at a whisper after the procedure. Her recovery was slow, and she shared with us her concern about the chances of never being able to use her voice to sing again with the children.

Little ones pick up on things quickly and Katie was no exception.

My friend and I were astonished as Katie walked over to Sister Ottley and said, "You don't have to worry, Sister Ottley. I have been praying to Heavenly Father. He is going to give you your voice back. I asked him to."

Katie didn't just pray that things might happen. She prayed that things would happen. At a young age, she felt that her Heavenly Father not only could but would intervene when her prayer was for a righteous desire. Such was the case when our old ugly blue car would not start. It would leave us sitting at the most inopportune times and just before we were ready to get out and walk, Katie would always plead, "Not yet mama, we didn't say a prayer."

The "blue bomb" as we affectionately called it, did not choke out its last fume until two weeks before graduation and that was only because Katie's prayers were no longer needed to get it running, as it was finally time to put it to rest.

As Katie grew older and went to school, she remained extremely shy and was not one to make numerous friends, but the friends she did have were close and loyal. Katie always looked for the good in others and went out of her way to please someone.

At age 18, her gifts of being spiritual and selfless would prove themselves again as Katie found herself facing her greatest challenge, the challenge of giving up Sammy. Sammy came into Katie's life and into her arms in the spring of 1993. I stood just outside the operating room as I heard his first cry. Our family cried, for we knew that our days with Sammy would be short. I knew I was never to watch him grow or to see his first steps. I also knew, being a Mother-Baby nurse, what my daughter was about to face as she gave up her little son for adoption. My heart ached for her.

It was only a few months earlier that Katie realized that she would be bringing a little one into this world. It had not been planned and she had decided that neither she nor Sammy's father were ready for such a responsibility. Scared and confused she had first contemplated the thoughts of abortion. A wise and caring church leader brought over a tape that was entitled "From His Arms, to My Arms, to Your Arms" and asked Katie if we could all listen to it together. Before the song was finished, we all had tears flooding our eyes. The song was powerful and helped my daughter to realize that even though mistakes do happen, they are complicated even more by abortion.

Katie then struck out to find a family for her baby. After much thoughtful study and concern, she chose a family that would allow an open adoption so that she might have part in Sammy's life. I felt concerned about her decision and really did not understand why.

As weeks passed, I continued to feel that the family Katie had chosen was not the right one. One morning I asked Katie what she thought would be the greatest gift she could give this baby.

Without hesitation Katie answered, "It would be the gift of knowing Heavenly Father like I do."

With love and concern, I asked her, "How will you be able to give that to him if this family does not share your belief about the Savior?"

Katie did not say much to me that day but before the week had ended, she came to me concerned. "How can I ever tell them that I have changed my mind?"

It was with prayer that Katie gained the strength to do what she knew she needed to do. Katie then chose a family who loved music and shared her spiritual beliefs. She chose a family who valued education. She chose a family that had already adopted a little boy that would become Sammy's brother. Thinking only of Sammy, she put aside the fact it would be a closed adoption.

We were happy that Katie had her baby by cesarean section. It would give her time to cradle him and love him as only a biological mother can, to look at his eyes, and hair and notice all of those little features that were part of her, and part of Sammy's father. Each day was exceedingly difficult for our family. Each day brought Katie closer to the day we knew was near. Each one of us with loving intentions told her that we would help her to raise Sammy if she could not follow through with her decision. She would always remind us how much she wanted her son to be raised with both a mother and father and have the joy of always being together, unlike her life of only knowing her father from across many miles.

The day Katie was to be discharged was one we all remember. For Katie, it was a day that she will never forget. As the time came closer, she felt the tugging of her heart strings. Confusion and fear were taking their toll and my sweet daughter asked that we all leave her room and let her be alone with her baby.

As Katie shared with me later, it was at that time that she knelt at her bedside and begged her Heavenly Father to help her know if she was doing the right thing. Katie said that as she petitioned her Father the most encompassing feeling of peace entered the room and encircled her. All doubt and worry abated. Calmness entered her heart, and peace took over her soul. She knew she was doing the right thing. From that moment on and even to this day she has always felt that she did the right thing.

Katie continued that morning saying her final farewell to her son Sammy. It was then that *she* took him into the nursery for she did not want her last memory of her little one to be the memory of him being taken out of her arms. She knew from that moment and for all time to come, that Sammy was truly a blessing to come from His arms, to be held shortly by her arms, to be picked up lovingly by theirs.

For Sammy, I Love You

Run Like the Wind

Jimmy learned to run before he was three. Baby sister Katie would cry out from being pushed or hit and poof! Jimmy ran so he wouldn't get a reprimand from mom or dad. Finally, we caught on that it was cute little Katie who always started the trouble. Big brother Jimmy was a saint to tolerate her pounding for so long and as often as he did. James Robert was my second born and second son. He was not as shy like little sister, and he was active. He was a typical boy. He loved G.I. Joe figures and he loved Legos.

I can tell you that it is important to observe your babies at an early age, for their gifts and talents are often demonstrated long before they enter school and sometimes before they are talking. Some babies listen to music while others get out in the middle of the living room floor and dance for any audience that will watch, even the family dog. Jimmy liked music. He liked to sing. Even at three he loved to dance. We did not know how well he could sing until his freshman year in high school when he announced after dinner that he had to go to the Spring Music Festival at the high school that same evening.

"Oh, by the way, mom, you don't have to come if you are

too tired," he announced.

What mother doesn't know that that means something is up? Such a secret he tried to hide. I almost fell out of my auditorium seat when they announced that Jim Knudson would be the lead soloist for all the Beach Boys songs. His beautiful tenor voice hit every one of those hard to reach notes. Boy, did we have a little talk after the concert. Moms shouldn't be the last to know things like that.

It was not music that was Jimmy's true passion, however. And it was not architectural design, regardless of the Legos. It was a gift that he would enjoy throughout his life. We saw the first glimpse of this talent when he was only five. Jimmy entered the "jog-a-thon" at his school to raise money for "Jerry's kids" with muscular dystrophy. We, of course, sponsored him thinking that he couldn't possibly run more than a lap or two being just five years old. Stunned parents we were when that little stinker ran 16 laps. He ran all 16 laps without stopping once. Sixteen laps was four miles. We were out $16, even though we were poor as church mice. We didn't care. We were so proud of him. Needless to say, our little Jimmy had several warm soaks in the bathtub over those next few days, to ease his aching five-year-old muscles.

When Jimmy entered high school, he joined the cross-country team. He broke his own fastest time over and over again and was able to go to district and state meets. I loved to watch him run. He would let the expected winner set the team's pace during the beginning of each race. He would stay right at the heels of the fastest runner. Then he would "kick it in," as we would all say, in the final two laps. The race would be on between Jimmy and the front runner.

At the end of Jimmy's sophomore year in high school, he participated in the "Hail to the Chiefs Meet," which was sponsored by the police units in the Pacific Northwest. Police officers and their immediate family members could run in the meet. I sat on the ledge of the Portland Pioneer Courthouse stairs along with another lady. She was there to watch her husband run. He was a sheriff. Over one thousand runners participated.

We were excited as they began to announce the names of those who were bounding over the finish line and we could see them just before they crossed over. I knew I would be sitting there for a while as Jimmy said he hoped he would finish somewhere in the middle as most of the runners there competed in marathons and triathlons. I thought it must have been a mistake as I heard my son's name called out as the eleventh placed runner, but I soon knew it was for real when he ran by, smiling and waving right there in front of me.

Jimmy lives in Alaska today. His scrapbook holds memories of the many races he has run. It also now holds pictures of the triathlons he has placed in. Sometimes he was top seated. There is pride in my heart for I know of the physical endurance and commitment it takes to keep your body fit. I also know that there is a closeness you feel with a higher power that lets you rise above the hurt and the exhaustion that try to defeat you. I believe in my heart that as you draw close to your maker in those moments, He will help you press on, to be near you as you run like the wind.

A Chance to Know You

This will be perhaps, the most difficult chapter of my life and of my book to write. The most profound lessons I would learn to this date in my lifetime would come from sharing my life with my son Anthony. Many people would say this chapter is too personal. Yes, it is very personal, life is personal. However, some of the mistakes we make can be far reaching. They will change the lives of those closest to us, and although we can repent for our part in those errors, we cannot always erase their spiraling consequences. With true repentance, the

Lord is there to forgive us and will "remember our sins no more." The most difficult challenge comes in forgiving ourselves.

When Tony was three, I met a man, fell in love, and was soon married.

My father, before walking me down the aisle, turned to me and said, "You don't have to do this. I will go out there and tell everyone you've changed your mind if you want me to." He was especially concerned, and as I found out years later, the concern was not just for his youngest daughter, but also for his three-year-old grandson.

The consequences of this marriage spiraled down leaving its effect on many for years to come. It became quite clear after only a few months that the love I was hoping for was not going to be given by my husband. He was rarely intimate or affectionate and the few times we were, I always became pregnant. In the short space of six years, we were to welcome five more children into our family. I loved Motherhood. I loved my little ones. I gave all the love I had to give to my children and focused on being a good mother. My husband was good to his children, and even though he had legally adopted my son Tony, most of our quarrels were about the way he disciplined Tony.

In 1982, and after two separations, our marriage ended. I truly grieved for my children. In a short time, their father moved miles away and they would never come to know "weekend visits" as some children do. Tony, however, was more angry than sad.

He asked at age nine if Jim was his biological father and when he found out that he was not, commented with tears in his eyes, "That is why he has treated me differently all this time."

Tony was 13 when the divorce was final. It was then that we moved from The Dalles, Oregon back to Portland, Oregon. Tony was having a difficult time. He had many angry feelings inside and did not know how to express them and often his actions were directed against his younger siblings.

Over and over again, I prayed to know what to do. It was a time of great change for all of us. I had made so many choices that were now affecting the lives of all my children that I did not want to put them through more. Again, and again as I prayed, I was impressed to let Tony meet his biological father. My parents were definitely against it, feeling that Tony would be hurt more if his father did not want to know his son. Every time I took my feelings to the Lord, I received a peaceful confirmation that it was the right thing to do.

I had not seen David since our last meeting, with the news that his parents would not allow us to marry. No longer would they acknowledge me or their grandchild to be. And with that David and I were to no longer see one another. There I was, 13 years later, calling Tony's grandmother. To my surprise she relinquished David's phone number.

How do you tell a man you would like him to meet his son? How do you ask a young man if he would like to meet his father? I had no idea. So, I did not ask. Am I sorry about that? Am I really sorry for being the instigator of what happened? Well...

I asked my son if he would like to go with me to have lunch at the new mall. At the same time, I asked David if he would like to join me at the mall to catch up on 13 years. Describing what we would be wearing and what kind of cars we would be driving, the date was set. I didn't think I would have a difficult time knowing who he was even from a distance because last I saw, David stood six foot four inches tall. I was so scared, but I reminded myself that I knew it was the right thing to do. Dave had already parked his car as he saw me and Tony pull into a parking space. My heart was pounding as he walked closer to the car. My son and I stepped out. Dave looked right at me with his head tilted in question. I then looked at my six-foot two-inch son with his head also tilted in question.

Tony spoke up first. "Mom, is he my dad?"

David looked at me, for across from him was standing the mirror image of himself, a young man with a contagious smile, long slender fingers, and sandy brown hair. I watched as they stood there looking at one another, a father and son meeting for the first time. Tony was the first to cry. I soon followed.

Dave did not ask if Tony was his son. He looked at me and joyfully stated, "This is my son."

I looked at them both with tears streaming down my cheeks and said, "I hope this is ok."

When Dave suggested we all sit down and have lunch together, I declined.

"Do you think you'll be ok alone together? Tony has waited for this for such a long time."

I knew they needed to be alone. They needed to catch up on so many years. I did not want to intrude on those most special moments, and with that, off they went to spend the day with one another. David had only four more years to be a father to his only son. As for Tony, I am sure those four short years made up for a lifetime.

7 EPILOGUE: TO KNOW HE IS THERE

I testify to those reading my words that our Heavenly Father is real. He loves us in a way that is hard to comprehend. He shares our joys and our sorrows. The key to feeling that love is to believe He exists. We must have faith to know He is there. Those seeds are planted in our hearts and minds simply at first. It may be an answer to a prayer. It may be a rescue to a safe haven. As those seeds take root, a foundation for faith is formed. Though rains may come, and winds might howl, strong roots will keep us anchored in place. Trials will only serve to make our testimonies grow stronger. As we share our testimonies of miracles, we help plant seeds for others. The veil that separates this life from the next is so thin, and often frail. I cannot imagine that a loving Heavenly Father would send us here to earth to find our way home alone. I do believe in angels. They have no wings. They are not always seen by our earthly eyes. They may be the whisperings of a loved one now gone, or a phone call from someone we love. I do believe it is through The Holy Ghost that these happenings can occur. He is a wonderful gift. It is up to us individually to plant our seeds in rich soil, so that we might keep Him with us always. With these final three stories...

Please, Know He Is There.

A Prompting

Jessica was loved, not only by her caring family, but by others as well. On a warm August day in 2000, a kind sister from our church assisted my sister Eileen in caring for Jessica. Jessica was bathed, and her beautiful long brown hair carefully braided. Jessica was then dressed in her pink rose bud shorty pajamas.

Jessica smelled fresh and sweet as Eileen sat close to her. With her night feeding completed, Eileen then embraced her little Jessica and held her tightly in her loving arms. On that evening, Eileen felt a closeness to her daughter she had never experienced before.

Stroking her long, braided hair, Eileen looked compassionately at Jessica's face. "I love you so very much," she whispered. Then positioning her carefully onto her bed, Eileen kissed Jessica gently on the cheek.

Eileen did not know that it would be her last kiss, but all evening she felt a closeness that was overwhelming, as though it was the first step in bringing her close to a final goodbye.

Jessica returned to Father in Heaven gently during the night. We later came to know she was happy as she prompted me repeatedly during a spiritual service, saying, "Tell mom I am here."

A Message from Tony

My son Anthony died in a tragic car accident at the age of 17. Low-lying fog made for a slippery and unseen curve in the road that Tony was unable to maneuver. He and his friend Robert left this world without suffering pain, as they passed on instantly. Tony, however, had unfinished business here upon this earth and it would not be long before he made that known.

Two years after Tony passed away, one of his closest friends, Darren was excited to see me at a church conference. Darren was going on his two-year mission soon. He told me how many times he and Tony had talked about going on a mission. Darren asked if Tony's endowment work had been completed in the Temple. (Endowments are promises an individual makes to our Heavenly Father about how they will righteously live their life, and blessings Heavenly Father bestows on the individual for time and all eternity.) Darren wanted to be the one, by proxy, to complete the endowment for Tony. I gave him permission, and then my address so we could keep in touch.

Months passed and I didn't hear from Darren. I did not have his address. The address I had given him had changed, as I had moved to Washington. About two years after Darren left for his mission, I started having dreams about my son. Each dream left me feeling that something was wrong. At the same time, my mother also began having the same dreams. We were always left with the impression that Tony was not at peace.

It was two and a half years from the time that Darren had left for his mission that I received the phone call. Darren was excited to be back and had been trying to find out where I had relocated. He had not been able to do Tony's endowment work because he needed more information to submit to the Temple. I now understood who had prompted our dreams. I was also excited to know that I would be able to be there in the Temple on the day his work would be completed.

We chose a beautiful afternoon to be at the Portland Temple. Traffic had made us late and we were all worried that we were going to miss the session, so filled with family and friends. I walked up to the greeting desk in the temple foyer.

The Temple worker at the front desk greeted me as though she had known me forever. "You must be Kim!"

I had not handed her my Temple recommend or Tony's Temple paperwork.

"He has been waiting for you all morning. He is so excited. You look exactly as he said you would," she disclosed.

The tears rushed to my eyes and I had to sit down because I was so overcome by the spirit. I cannot describe to you the feelings that overwhelmed me for a time.

"You must hurry," she said. "The session is about to start. I will tell them to wait. Your son is so handsome and so tall. Kim, I have never seen a young man quite so happy."

My son was six feet five at the time of his passing. He was indeed handsome. I could not see him as the Temple greeter had been able to, but to feel his spirit and to know he was happy was enough. I look forward to the time when we reminisce about that day...together.

Going Home

I knew that Mr. Otto Roder's story was to be the final story of my book. I knew it in the space of only a few short, but most wonderful hours after meeting him. I would not learn until almost one year later how significant his story would become. His story when read by others would be a magnificent testimony of the power of our Heavenly Father. Once again, our loving Father would pour down His blessings on a man who had the faith to know He was there.

I must take you back to our first meeting. I introduced myself to Mr. Roder there in his hospital room. I told him my name was Kim and that I would be his nurse for that day.

He outstretched his hands to take mine with both of his

and stated, "I shall not call you Kim. I will call you 'my dear' or perhaps 'my love' but do not take it personally for that is who I am."

I liked him immediately. I did a simple nursing assessment and then asked him what his pain level was on a scale of one to ten.

He was calm so when he answered, "Maybe a ten or eleven."

I was confused. Drug-seeking patients can chat on their cell phone or with a smile say, "I'm at a ten." Mr. Roder was a man with cancer. He did not show his pain. That changed drastically when I asked him if he needed assistance to use the restroom while I was there in his room.

It took a while to help him pivot his legs over the side of his bed. His smile was replaced with agony. Each position shift left him grimacing with pain. I placed his walker in front of him so he could stand. He was very tall. It took all his strength to stand up straight. Getting him situated in the bathroom was every bit as painful. I soon realized that a "ten" was a severe underestimation of his actual pain. It was out of control. I gave him privacy and went to the medication room for morphine. I logged onto the computer and looked at his diagnosis. I knew he had cancer. I did not know that it had invaded all of the long bones in his body. It became my goal to keep Mr. Roder comfortable. It became his goal to make me happy.

He was kind. He was hopeful. He knew his prognosis was not a positive one. Discharge planners arranged for all the things he would need at home to keep him comfortable, from an adjustable bed to oral doses of morphine. It was a difficult time at best. Mr. Roder's daughter was a gem and helped to keep the atmosphere as calm as she could. Her stepmother, Mrs. Roder, was having a most difficult time. All the changes that were taking place became overwhelming for her. Mr. Roder was concerned for both of them. That is who he was.

Though Mr. Roder's reason for hospitalization was for pain control and to arrange for a comfortable level of care at his home, his goal was to trust in the powers he knew. He and I shared spiritual stories. We talked about the power of prayer. He was most definitely close to his Heavenly Father. He was not angry about his pain. He was not angry with God. He stated that the purpose for our existence here on this earth was to help others know of his goodness. He thanked God for his trials and only hoped he could endure well, what was ahead of him. Mr. Roder radiated a Christ-like love for people. I felt it every time I entered his room.

When it was time for me to go home, I actually hated the fact that my shift was over. Though my day had been busy and my shift had been difficult, I felt a bit of heaven each time I entered Mr. Roder's room. I told Mr. Roder's daughter that her dad's story was to be the final chapter in my book. I was happy to have their permission. I was sad as I left the hospital that evening.

Months passed by and I had to put work at the hospital aside due to hip pain. I focused for a time on finishing my book. I thought of Mr. Roder often and wondered if he had returned home to Heavenly Father. After weeks of editing stories, I wanted Mr. Roder's story to be just right.

I hated to make the call. I had been putting it off for days. How do you ask someone if their father is still living? I was almost relieved when the phone recording said, "please leave a message." I did just that. I left a message. A couple of days later I missed the call that said, "Oh yes, Kim. Dad is still with us. You can call me back, but you might want to call Dad yourself." She left his number. This time I was eager to make the call.

"Oh, Kim, dear. How are you?" Mr. Roder said. "I have been waiting for your call." The same cheerful voice was heard, for it was Mr. Roder after all. "Did my daughter tell you?" he asked.

I was in awe as he spent the next few minutes catching up, telling me what had happened.

"You know I wasn't afraid to die, Kim. I know where I am going," he said.

He told me of the great concern he had for his wife. He

told me he had prayed often for the Lord to give him more time so that he could be with her longer. I know that he would have loved to have more time, even if it meant time in pain. His prayers were not for himself. His prayers were for her. He continued to tell me how his PSA (a measurement used in prostate cancer) was now at 2.3 and no longer at 1,000. I was amazed when he told me he was no longer on any medications, for he had left the hospital on high doses of morphine.

Words could not express my joy for him. I told him so. He then told me what we both already knew.

It will never matter what trial we go through. It does not matter if the trial we face is from the result of our own poor choices or if it is placed in front of us for our growth. How we go through our trials makes all the difference in the world. Satan would want us to feel deep despair as we face them. He would want us to lose hope and not be able to pick ourselves up again.

I hope I will always remember Mr. Otto Roder. I hope I can remember his example, to smile sweetly through pain and continue to honor our Father even when this life tips me upside down. I hope I will continue to remember that the "things" of this earth hold no treasure that I can take home. Who I am as a person and what example I have been to others is what matters most. When Mr. Roder does leave this life, I will hold close to my heart, the person that he was and the example that he was for me. He gave me a wonderful gift, one that will not fade with time. Mr. Roder shared his testimony that God is real and proved with prayer what tremendous faith he had...

"To know God is there."

(Written with permission from a most wonderful man who was permitted to stay two more years before returning to his "Forever home")

There is no greater gift than *To Know He Is There*

ABOUT THE AUTHOR

Kimberly Larraine now lives a quiet, unassuming life in a small Oregon community. Although she feels that becoming a nurse was a great accomplishment under the circumstances she faced, she feels her greatest "accomplishment" is being a grandma to 36 children. She's always loved the arts and loves storytelling, not reading books but telling aloud her own creations. She was a children's music instructor for her church for over 30 years. Another thing that gives her feelings of great joy is the title of THE Cookie Lady in whatever community she has resided, and in serving other people.

And one day you might have the pleasure of reading her children's stories.